My 60 Years Hunting Michigan Whitetails

My 60 Years
Hunting
Michigan Whitetails

By

Kenneth L. Peterson

My 60 Years Hunting Michigan Whitetails

What The Deer Taught Me

Copyright © 1997 by Kenneth L. Peterson
First printing 1997
Printed in the United States of America

Cover photo by Kenneth L. Peterson
Cover design by Kay Richey
Layout and design by Kay Richey
Electronically created camera-ready copy by
  KLR Communications, Inc.
  POB 192
  Grawn, MI 49637

Art illustrations by
  Clark N. Sullivan
  4288 Staunton Dr.
  Swartz Creek, MI 48473

My 60 Years Hunting Michigan Whitetails, What The Deer Taught Me By Kenneth L. Peterson
Whitetail Deer / Michigan - North America

ISBN 0-9658661-0-6 Softcover

Acknowledgments

My files are bulging with research and management reports and with statistics - all supplied by people who wanted to keep me on the straight and narrow. I am especially mindful of the parts played by Ilo H. Bartlett, David Arnold, Edward Langenau Jr., Louis J. Verme and John J. Ozoga, all of whom spent much time with me over a 40-year period. Then, too, this book was launched with the advice and counsel, and encouragement, of David and Kay Richey, who gave needed support.

Dedication

This book is dedicated to Tom Huggler who urged me to write it and to my hunting buddy, Clark Sullivan, wildlife artist and illustrator of this book who, fortunately, nagged me until the book was finished.

Contents

Prologue

It comes with the season, slowly, imperceptibly, but surely — that transition in the inner being of the deer hunter each fall. It comes as the days get shorter and the nights become cooler. There's a hint of what is in the offing as songbirds begin to flock and change their spring and summer songs to chatty fall gabble. The change comes wrapped in a seemingly different smell that emanates from the pre-autumn landscape.

Maybe it is kicked off by the first changes in leaf color, those early-changing shrubs and prematurely changing tree leaves. Perhaps the ripening of wild fruit sets it off. Or is it simply seeing what man has sowed reach its fullness in time and go under the sickle?

Whatever it is, whatever this transition that seems to grip the deer hunter, it causes a stir in his breast — an awakening, a response to changes in the outdoor world that seem to ride with the wind.

Yes, fall creates a new purpose for the hunter just as it seems to instill a new urgency in the activities of wildlife.

Something wells within the hunter — perhaps a sensation not unlike that of the lion, which, like the hunter, lives for a time in seeming harmony with its prey and then breaks that temporary truce and relaxes again only when its belly is full.

When the hunter goes on the prowl, he answers an urge — an instinct that begins to grip him. But he goes not just to fill his belly, for many would go hungry if they did. He goes to quiet that inner restlessness.

He pursues his prey not for survival, but to placate those stirrings fanned by the changes in seasons. For this hunter, it is a fulfillment. He thrills in the presence of deer. He spends hours watching them. He photographs, feeds and fondles them. He worries over them and feels for them when they perish.

Yet he stalks his prey deliberately and intensely. When he kills, he does it thinkingly and quickly. But where the kill is vital to the wild predator, the quest is of the utmost importance to this hunter. He kills only because, he too, savors the meat of his prey.

So a hunter need not be ashamed of being a predator, for that is what he is — that is his heritage. When his season arrives, he is ready to assert that practiced, skillful predatory relationship. But it is a momentary thing. The hot blood cools quickly. The ritual is short.

In the end, the hunter has relived an ancient role and he is full of memories. He is satiated.

Introduction

This book is not intended to be a primer on hunting white-tailed deer. Nor is it a roundup of popular information on whitetail hunting. It is just what the title says — an account of my experiences when hunting deer for 60 years and my deductions from those encounters.

In a sense, it traces the deer-hunting education of a person who has spent a lifetime hunting. The knowledge related is personal unless otherwise stated. However, having been trained in wildlife management and having had a 30-year-plus association with wildlife biologists, the author feels his experiences have been well grounded and augmented.

The book may corroborate findings of other writers, but it also may refute statements made by some simply because those assertions do not jibe with this writer's experience. In my quest for knowledge, I have tried seemingly crazy approaches to deer and deer hunting touted by other hunters either out of curiosity or merely to put the ideas behind me.

The intent of the book is to relate enough experiences with deer to draw the kinds of conclusions that will help the novice get a grasp on deer behavior and hunting tactics. And it is my hope that the experienced hunter will be able to relate to and enjoy the hunting tales and perhaps broaden his knowledge of deer and deer hunting.

By the same token, this writing does not pretend to be all-knowing or the last word in deer hunting. For one thing, it relates only the experiences of the author. Secondly, whitetails still are teaching this hunter little things that enhance his enjoyment of deer and deer hunting.

How dreary deer hunting would be if one had nothing more to learn.

The Michigan Deer Story

"Click. Click. Click."

The sounds were slight. But, in the quiet of the dusk, I could hear them. I could hear them coming closer to the edge of the swamp near Grayling. And I knew the sound.

The tiny noises were made by deer moving through the thick balsams that edged the swamp. Deer moving methodically down trails through the trees were breaking dead, dry twigs protruding from the trunks. Deer were heading out from the Tyler Branch swamp into the hills for the night and I was watching the runway they were taking.

Shortly, the head of a doe was framed by trees at the edge. The animal had stopped, as usual, to survey the open ground before leaving cover. It glanced back and then moved out into the relatively open country, country still bearing the impressions of the Big Wheels that carried the last of the pine — white and red — out of the hills to the banking grounds near Hartwick Pines.

It was country now forested, for the most part, with second-growth maples and aspen, a scattering of choke cherry, pin cherry, black cherry, occasional jack pines, staghorn sumac and hazelnut. And it was terrain supporting raspberry, blackberry and blueberry. Add witch-hazel, grey dogwood, bracken fern and a "forest" of blackened pine stumps. And add farms two miles to the north. This was the Michigan deer country I roamed as a youth.

17

The spot the deer vacated at the swamp edge was almost immediately filled by another bald head. That doe paused, then followed the first deer. She was replaced by a third deer, and a fourth. They continued to come, head-to-tail, until 22 deer had exited the swamp and walked by my stand.

Not a "horn" was among them. But I had hunted enough years by then to get used to such an evening performance. This was in 1939 and Crawford County, where I lived and did most of my hunting at that time, was among the northern lower Michigan counties that were overrun by whitetails. Others were parts of Roscommon, Ogemaw, Montmorency, Alpena and Oscoda counties. In the days before the hunter-orange rule these central counties attracted a horde of redcoats.

In the hours I had spent that day scouring Crawford County's cut-over sections, I saw lots of deer — saw them in twos and threes or fours. One group of seven almost ran over me even though the country was so sparsely timbered they had to see me. (Many of the open areas have persisted and modern lumbering has created many cut-over — hence, open — areas.)

By the end of the day, I had counted 55 deer — every one of them identified as a doe or fawn, for there were no antlers long enough to see with my three-power field glasses. I had expected to see from 25 to 50 deer, so the big count was surprising only because 22 of those deer had herded up.

Seeing lots of deer was typical of the times when I was a teenager. The state had gone through one surge in the deer population before 1900 as the timber was cut and, now, in the 1930s, was experiencing another.

Prior to 1850, according to a paper by Ilo H. Bartlett, the state's deer expert who watched deer get into trouble in the 1930s, the herd was relatively small north of Bay City. Most of the area was covered by virgin conifers and hardwood.

Loggers cured that in the last half of the 19th Century. The timber was replaced by the kind of brush and vegetation that deer like. This combined with natural openings, swamps and marshes to create good deer country. And the deer thrived — too well for their own good.

Deer became a convenient source of food for the lumberjacks, opening up jobs for people like my grandfather who shot game for lumber camps in Kalkaska County. Commercial hunting for the big-city markets took thousands of animals annually. Sport hunting also became popular, although sportsmen did not make big inroads into the herd. Adding to whitetail woes were the successive wildfires that burned through the slash left by lumberjacks. Hunting and the plow routed deer from southern lower Michigan, the early stronghold of the state's deer herd. Few were left in the south by 1880.

That's the year the early herd reached a peak, Bartlett writes. More than 100,000 deer were killed and shipped to the market. After 1880, what farming did in the south, wildfires did in the north. Fires burned year after year in the slash left by loggers. Winter food became scarce and deer declined until the low level of 1850 was again reached and surpassed. By 1900, records show, there were only 50,000 deer in Michigan — even fewer than in the 1850s.

By 1890, Michigan's great timber industry had peaked and had pretty well diminished by 1910. The deer might have done better, but hunters harassed them all year before 1859 and no license was required until 1895. In that year, hunters still could take five deer annually. It wasn't until 1915 that the limit was cut to one deer a year; then, in 1921, the one-buck law was imposed. That was the year the state Department of Conservation was organized. (It became the Department of Natural Resources in 1968.) Finally, the season was shortened in 1925 to Nov. 15-30, the current dates.

Getting the one-buck law passed came after much argument despite the bad times the deer herd was experiencing. The state game warden at the time testified that it wasn't easy for hunters to pass up taking "a nice fat doe." Because it wasn't, it took 12 years to get legislative approval of the one-buck law. No wonder the Department of Natural Resources marks the first couple of decades of the 20th century as lean ones, indeed, for the Michigan whitetail. Only a semblance of herd recovery was noted by 1920.

With the limit cut to one buck annually, deer were given a chance to respond to the regrowth of Michigan forests. The doe became sacred as hunters attributed a burgeoning herd to the protection afforded females. Where it took a dozen years of campaigning to get hunters to give up shooting does and support passage of the one-buck law, it took even longer in later years to get agreement that the herd should be kept within bounds of its habitat by shooting antlerless deer on a limited basis.

Hunters tended to forget that protection of the doe, important as that was, was not the sole reason the herd rebounded. Thousands of acres of budding new forest was finally given a chance to grow when the state gained control over forest fires. Be mindful, too, that closure of much of the Lower Peninsula also helped the deer herd. It wasn't until 1948 that the entire state was opened to deer hunting again — for the first time since 1891.

Fortunately for me, I started hunting whitetails on the heels of the modern resurgence of the herd. A combination of protection and the end of massive forest fires set the stage for the herd comeback. Still, forest fires were common each summer in the 1930s. Where fires did occur, they kept new vegetation down.

In 1930, the healing regrowth still was so short in the Crawford County uplands near Lovells where we hunted snowshoe rabbits that I could see for a half mile despite the fact I was only 8. I will never forget the day my older brother emptied his .22 repeating rifle - all 16 shots - at a rabbit running through the brush in that rolling country. Even after he emptied the gun, we could still see the fleeing bunny. The country was so open that I could overlook hundreds of acres of food deer could easily reach.

Deer were able to benefit because the state was developing fire-fighting equipment that enabled it to reach fires more quickly and get them under control more easily. At the outset of the '30s, fighting fires was part of life where I lived. I could see smoke in the air at some time just about every summer. I remember helping fight grass and brush fires before I was 10 years old.

20

MICHIGAN DEER KILL 1935-1961 , GUN

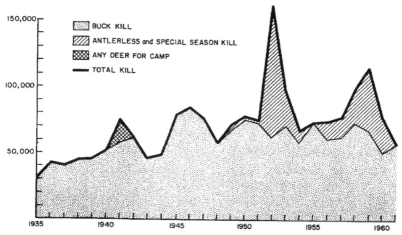

Early records show how buck kill climbed, then leveled out. Only by shooting antlerless deer could the DNR achieve a large kill increase. (Michigan Department of Conservation graph.)

But these were good years for a budding deer hunter, for there were lots of deer and lots of elbow room. When I paid $2.25 for a license to shoot my first buck in 1937, the state estimates only 154,790 sportsmen and sportswomen hunted deer that year. I was one of just 39,760 rifle hunters who bagged a buck — a statewide success rate of about 25 percent. (The smattering of camp deer and archery kills was not counted in those figures.)

But we were headed for the days when one in five males 15 and older would hunt deer with a gun. Firearm licenses doubled between 1920 and 1930 (to 76,500) and would double again by 1946. License sales increased 1.8 times from 1946 to 1968. In the next 10 years, sales went to 821,000. Just three years later, the total was 971,239 — the record high.

When all of the elements favorable to an expanding deer herd came together, I think Michigan had what biologists call a deer population explosion. I never heard Bartlett or other biologists call it that, but the rapid expansion of the herd fitted the classic description. At least that is what I saw in north-central lower Michigan in my early deer hunting years. Biologists still argue

21

over the size of the herd in the late 1930s, many who were in the field disagreeing with Lansing that the herd was as small as official figures now put it. Individual experiences obviously differed just as they do today and some counties, of course, had more deer than others.

Where Bartlett estimated a herd of 1.17 million in 1938, today biologists claim the herd was only a little over half that size then. I can only say that I was always dodging does and fawns when I began deer hunting. And I think the herd might have been more heavily concentrated where my family hunted because our area was among the first to suffer serious food shortages, the club country to the northeast being the first. The northern two-thirds of the state contained most of the deer in those days. Southern lower Michigan had few deer at the time — in fact was closed to hunting. The north half of the Lower Peninsula harbored the bigger share of the herd.

The Upper Peninsula had fewer deer because logging was less extensive and fires less severe. The size of local herds depended on logging. As a result, deer in one area could be starving while deer in another would be thriving because of the cutting. Bartlett said (in 1943) logging had been continuous in the U.P., but varied in volume over the years. Loggers still are taking virgin timber there. Bartlett said in his appraisal of the U.P. that it had been possible to find swamps across the length of the U.P. in various stages of growth because of the nature of the logging. Deer still depend on logging there, and the modern increase in cutting has favored a growth in the deer herd.

When I was old enough to drive in 1939, it fell to me to show visitors deer. That meant driving out to the Hanson State Game Refuge, which coincided with the original military reservation southwest of Grayling. It was typical to count 100 deer in an evening's drive through the parade grounds, rifle ranges and other open areas. The one-buck law was working.

In the spring, I picked the Hartwick Pines area, where deer would come out of the river swamps to feed on exposed hillsides along the highway. One time I counted 125 deer on one small

George Heany serves as one essential in deer camp - the camp cook.

hillside. Those hillsides now are timbered with 50-year-old hardwoods.

Where I could see up to 50 or more deer daily during deer season in the late '30s, I could see only about a half dozen a day in the 1950s. My daily sightings dropped that low even though biologists now say the deer herd had expanded to more than 900,000 by 1953.

But my hunting was confined to counties where the huge deer herd experienced heavy winter losses. Cedar swamps were hit hard by hungry wintering deer. In the '30s and '40s I had some favorite swamps for hunting snowshoes. Cedar was so thick I had to drop to my knees and look up rabbit trails to see very far through the ground-hugging cedar. But the practice netted me a few extra rabbits because I often caught one sitting on a trail.

By the mid-1940s, those swamps were almost barren of snowshoes. The cedar had been browsed head-high and the swamps were so open that deer no longer flocked to them. In fact, herds of deer no longer were evident in my hunting area in the late '40s. Among the tell-tale signs were the fading trails deer once used as they headed into the hills from the swamps. When I first started hunting, these trails resembled cow paths. They were deeply cut into the sod and were chopped up by sharp hooves. Grass had about obliterated those deer trails by the '50s. The signs told me our local deer were in trouble long before the DNR had nerve enough to declare an antlerless deer season. At the time, we all thought it came too late.

The DNR was preaching herd control in the late '30s, but the tentative steps it took in the 1940s to whittle the doe population by holding limited seasons satisfied no one. Then it went overboard.

In 1952, the Natural Resources Commission went further than biologists recommended by opening the entire northern half of the Lower Peninsula to killing a deer of either sex during the last three days of the season. It cured the over abundance — to put it mildly — of deer in many areas. But the DNR received such a bad image from allowing the huge doe kill that it still suffers in some respects, despite the good deer hunting nimrods enjoy.

Bear in mind that the number of deer hunters jumped from 376,000 in 1951 to 455,000 in 1952 because of that three-day season. The deer kill went from 81,600 in 1951 to 162,160 in 1952. The doe season was restricted to northern lower Michigan, where only 2,270 special-permit deer were allowed in 1951. That jumped to 95,810 — most of them does and fawns — in 1952. People called it a slaughter, and it seemed so because that deer kill was concentrated in the deer hot spots in only one-third of the state.

No wonder deer hunters were angry at the DNR. By 1952, Mother Nature had trimmed the herd so well where I hunted that the special season wreaked havoc on the deer. In one tiny strip of swamp along a river I counted 11 bloody drag trails ending at the trail road that ran along the swamp. The next fall, this area was almost void of deer tracks and we quit hunting it. There was snow on the ground during the special season and the country I hunted was criss-crossed with red trails before it was over.

Subsequently, "seeing" deer became a big issue with hunters. My drives to show tourists deer became sad disappointments. I remember how hunters were irked when the game biologist for the area insisted "there are lots of deer." It wasn't until the early 1960s that I heard the same biologist admit to a sportsmen's group: "You are right, we don't have as many deer as we used to have." By the mid-1960s DNR biologists were conducting deeryard tours to explain why the herd was so low. And some of those tours were in the U.P., where no wide-open season was held in 1952.

The herd was estimated at 1,025,000 in 1951. By 1961, it had dwindled to 672,000. But it dropped even more later in the '60s and hit a low of 446,000 by 1970. The 1952 kill had opened the way to heavy antlerless kills during the 1960s and the drastic drop in the deer population was not lost on deer hunters, including this one.

The furor over setting antlerless seasons became loud and

long during the late 1950s and all through the 1960s after the herd failed to rebuild in the face of antlerless seasons. I remember one particularly bitter session of the state Natural Resources Commission (meetings were tumultuous for years) when it was debating antlerless regulations for 1971. Faced with rebellious deer hunters who tied up proceedings for hours and the threat of a legislative override of its actions, the commission agreed to a 32 percent reduction in antlerless permits.

In November that year, Merrill L. (Pete) Petoskey, newly named chief of the Wildlife Division, promised upset sportsmen that Michigan would have a deer herd of a million animals by 1980.

That sounded pretty bold, since it meant more than doubling the herd. But by being conservative in killing antlerless deer (which pleased at least some outspoken field biologists), the DNR was able to reach its goal by 1978. By 1981, the kill exceeded 200,000 and success reached more than 23 percent. Deer management in the '80s would prove that Michigan hunters no longer had to fight antlerless hunting and did not have to be content with a limited deer harvest. (Other controversies popped up, however, such as baiting — an issue treated in this book.)

My early years — that I thought were so good — were a marked contrast to 1994, when I started this book. The DNR reported 684,220 regular season hunters that year. Firearms hunters took 173,840 bucks. For all seasons combined, the take was an estimated 363,910 deer. This was fewer than the record take of an estimated 452,490 harvested in 1989 — but still a good season. The success rate on bucks, however, was not much better than it was in 1937. It was 25 percent then and 23 percent in 1994.

There's a good reason for the big kills in the late 1980s and early 1990s. The deer herd had increased to an estimated two million in 1989 and again in 1995. The increase reflected, in part, the increased cutting of northern forests. The ratio of bucks had risen because of managed antlerless kills and as a result of a booming southern Michigan herd. Deer in the farmbelt had been gradually increasing until there were more deer there and more deer killed there annually than in the U.P.

Perhaps more significant is the growth in archery hunting, which I think can be attributed to the invention of the compound bow, a bow that just about anyone can pull with comfort and ease. The same cannot be said of the traditional bow. So the compound bow brought a whole new element into archery hunting — the rifle hunter, looking for a way to be in the deer woods longer.

Where there was archery hunting (for bucks only) in only two counties (Iosco and Newaygo) in 1937, archers in 1989 had 2 1/2 months to shoot any kind of deer in the state and could buy licenses to kill both a doe and a buck. And there were archers. In 1970, the number of bowhunters had grown to 68,540. By 1994, the number actually hunting had soared to 340,990. And they took 112,490 deer, upping this to 113,130 in 1995. This was more than rifle hunters took in some years a few decades ago. By 1994, firearms hunters also could buy two buck licenses. Add to that various special seasons making it possible for a properly licensed hunter to take up to 12 deer. The DNR still was not satisfied in 1996 that enough antlerless deer were being shot.

The 1994 buck kill was to me of outstanding significance. Starting about 1963 I wrote about the fortunes of deer hunter and herd for 23 years. For years the Wildlife Division chiefs would rub their hands in glee if sportsmen killed 100,000 deer in a single season. Presumably that was the goal because the annual take in most years was well below that for decades. For years the only way the DNR seemingly could achieve a significant increase in the annual deer kill was to increase the number of antlerless deer allowed. It was thought for years that hunters were taking just about all of the bucks they physically could. But, after Petoskey turned things around, it was demonstrated that nimrods could not only take more deer, but could take many more bucks annually as well. Since the mid-1980s it has become apparent that the deer herd is making a third resurgence. And hunters like it.

I had my fill of low deer numbers and high hunter counts by

1960, so when I got a chance that year to move to a happier hunting ground — the U.P. — I moved. But I still remember my last season in Crawford County. Despite hunting in an area where I knew every deer trail, I hunted 2 1/2 days without seeing a deer. I found the same low deer count in other north-central counties.

By 1961, the state counted 420,000 deer hunters, 269,000 of them in northern lower Michigan where I hunted. Thirty years later, there were 750,000 in the state. Good reason for shifting to the U.P. But I went back for a visit one year. My brother posted me on a hillside and told me he would be back. As daylight came, I could hardly stand sitting there. In my view were 12 orange coats, all within rifle shot. By contrast the U.P. was almost unreal. I could hunt all day and never see another hunter.

I had 17 great years in that camp, which straddled the line between Delta and Menominee counties. We had about four square miles of timber and swamps to hunt. It was not ideal deer country, but in the radius deer would travel were both abandoned and working farms as well as logging operations. I saw few deer on a daily basis even though I walked all day, probing at least four square miles. But the buck-doe ratio was in great contrast to that in my old hunting area. If I saw a deer at all, there was a 50-50 chance of it being a buck. Every buck I shot at that camp was either alone or with another buck. So why should I get excited about not seeing a lot of does? I might have been seeing only six does daily in my old territory, but seeing six deer in the U.P. would mean seeing at least one buck. The last year I hunted in that Delta-Menominee camp I saw only three deer in a week. But they were all bucks, one a 200-pounder.

Hunting that rugged land — I also hunted Iron, Baraga and Marquette counties — was such a great experience that I helped build a deer camp and still hunt there. I can usually count on taking at least one buck, but I think the wild land that I hunt is the great attraction. It is enough to make me resist going back south even though statistics tell me the buck-doe ratio is better below the straits in at least some places. Some years ago a study in one county where only bucks could be taken showed a buck-doe ratio of 50-1. More recent research in the same county has shown a ratio of one buck to four antlerless deer.

Ed Langenau, the state's deer specialist until April 1, 1997, says he would like to see bucks make up 35 percent of the herd. He agrees with me that the percentage of bucks taken, relative to the deer population, has been increasing over the last several years.

The buck-doe ratio over the years cannot be represented as a straight line relationship, according to Langenau. During the first years of the century, he said, the buck harvest represented 2-4 percent of the fall herd. In the next 50 years, he said the buck kill represented about 7.8 to 9.5 percent of the herd. In the last decade, a plateau of 9.3 percent (in 1984) to 24 percent (in 1988) was reached. The ratio of bucks dropped to 13.1 percent in 1993. The most these figures do is demonstrate how difficult it is to suggest the casual factors that operate on an annual basis to create the buck-doe ratio, Langenau declared.

There are a number of things to look at, he said. One is an antlerless harvest that increases fawn survival and, hence, the recruitment of bucks to the herd. It's possible, he said, that increased bag limits and longer seasons have reduced poaching and waste. Thirdly, there are more deer in southern lower Michigan where the buck-doe ratio is higher and where there is more recruitment of 1 1/2-year-old bucks.

In fact, southern lower Michigan is the bright spot in modern Michigan deer hunting. Its herd has soared in late years, so much so that the deer kill has exceeded that of all of the Upper Peninsula, which once produced the second largest kill and was long the fabled home of large bucks. Those southern counties now produce greater hunting for huge bucks, including record-class animals. And, where it might take only a 2-3 years to grow a big buck in the farmbelt, it takes about five years to produce a trophy in the U.P., the DNR says.

When I was a youngster, the deer season always brought excitement because I would join the other kids and watch the cars coming into Grayling enroute home with their bucks.

29

Wherever they stopped — gas stations or restaurants — we were there to gaze in awe at the huge antlers. Most of those big bucks came from the U.P. The antlers were massive and carried 10 points or more. But the story is different now, with most of the biggest bucks coming from the Lower Peninsula.

Commemorative Bucks of Michigan, official keeper of Michigan Big Game Records, lists top bucks in many ways. One list is of the top 300 bucks taken by firearms. Of the top 10 animals on the all-time list, only three came from the U.P. But the significant story that list tells is that only three of those top 10 were taken back in the days I talk about — 1947 and earlier. The rest are "modern" bucks

One change that affects modern hunting is the increase in hunting pressure, causing a higher exploitation of bucks. Hunters have better access to deer territory, Langenau said, because of an increase in forest trails and use of off-road vehicles. And he thinks there is more competition to find secluded country. That may be true, but a good share of the big bucks are taken in lower Michigan farm country. They essentially are "backyard" bucks — deer protected by the large expanses of private land they inhabit.

I live and have hunted in that farm atmosphere. When I have done so, the sounds of dogs barking, cattle lowing, back doors slamming and parents calling children indoors have made me feel utterly out of place — not to mention somewhat foolish for expecting to kill a buck under such circumstances.

So I drive 400 miles north to Marquette County, where any sound I hear is made by a wild creature, a place where sometimes the silence is deafening. I drive that far even though bucks skirt my front yard and leave rubbed branches and scrapes just to mock me. But I hunt in wild country where my success is not dependent on other hunters pushing deer my way. It's a place I can roam like I did as a youth, checking deer trails for good sign, for scrapes and for rubbed bushes and trees. It's a place where I do not have to be concerned by how many deer I see in a day, for all I look for is just one — the buck I might claim as mine.

Although I see few deer, I know there are twice as many in the U.P. as there were in the "good old days." All I have to do is shift my hunting spot if I want to see 25 to 50 deer daily. Michigan has the deer to satisfy almost any desire hunters may have, with the exception of a few places that just don't produce in the face of modern hunting pressure. So I hunt where there are few deer but where the buck ratio is high enough to fill a hunter with anticipation. I guess that is what hunting is all about. It's about anticipation fired by all of the memories of past hunts and the possibility of recreating one of them just one more time.

Chapter 2

Learning About Deer

The sun was about to disappear behind the tree tops across the road from the farm and the farm lad had learned what that meant. So he turned his eyes toward the 40 acres Granddad used for a pasture south of the farm. Sure enough. One deer, two deer, three white-tailed deer bounded over the south pasture fence and cut across the corner. They leaped the east fence with the same effortless ease and disappeared into the hardwoods.

The youngster, who spent more time in the woods surrounding the farm than working, turned his eyes to the woodlot which jutted into the hayfield on the 40 acres of working farm. Soon, one after another, the three deer jumped the south farm fence into a little corner of hay meadow created by the intrusion of the woodlot. They stopped there to nose about, but they wouldn't stay there long. They would soon cross the woodlot to feed in the cornfield on the north side of the woods.

The performance of the three deer that summer was repeated night after night at the same time, and this ritual probably was the beginnings of my education about deer, for I was that farm lad. Observing those deer and other wildlife around the farm in Crawford County was the highlight of the my summer vacation. The deer in that country and I were well acquainted, for Granddad let his cows roam the woods and I was the one elected to drive them back every day for milking. That meant driving the woods roads and firelines and listening for the cowbells. The bells took

33

me many places in surrounding sections of land, among them the South Waterhole, the Devil's Elbow waterhole and the North Waterhole. The cows and I were not the only visitors to these watering places. Deer trails chopped deep into the sod led to them and betrayed a large population of whitetails in that country.

In those summers throughout the 1930s, that whole country north of the Alexander Lakes became first my playground and then my hunting ground.

Before I got blood in my eye, I was content to "play" with the deer, tracking them and stopping worried does in their tracks by imitating tiny fawns. Then, when I swapped my shotgun for a rifle, I realized I knew something important about deer. I knew where their trails were and I knew that they did not show up at the farm by chance. The evening show was a habitual performance, their nightly feeding foray. Wherever else they may have fed or traveled during the day, at this time — when the sun touched the tree tops — their schedule called for them to be at the farm to feed.

Those whitetails were as dependable as the sun dipping behind the treetops west of the farm, something I remembered when I started out hunting those farm-oriented deer. I learned, too, as I sneaked into Granddad's "secret" blackberry patch south of the pasture that those three deer (and probably others I hadn't seen) had created a noticeable north-south trail leading up to the pasture. It was almost as well defined as one of the many trails made by Granddad's cows. Deer trails started making sense, they were used for specific purposes — one of them being to feed.

When I tried to find out where those trailmakers came from, I learned something else — where they hung out during the day. It was apparent those deer sought secure places when not feeding. It was just as evident that runways connected the two places. And that meant that runways would be key places to expect to see deer. The trail through Granddad's blackberry patch became more significant — it was a place to collect a buck. And I did just that!

In the light of 60 years of deer hunting, it is obvious that I had learned something about the two major requirements of deer. Those are food and security. It didn't take long to realize that runways connected the two and that runways were the places to hunt. I had learned the basics of where to hunt deer.

As I checked out those runways, I learned something else — deer rub their antlers as they walk the trails. I didn't know all the reasons why, but I didn't have to be much of a sleuth to reason that trails showing rubbings were the trails to hunt. I also learned how to distinguish successive years of rubbings. I decided, and the bucks proved me right, that the best runways to watch were those bucks used year after year — as demonstrated by those rubs. I was beginning to refine my knowledge.

Walking those runways taught that deer in that country sel- dom ranged far when they fed, seldom more than a mile once they found a place that suited their needs. A half mile north of the farm, my cousin hunted deer that never saw my Granddad's fields. They ranged to other farms. It suggested to me that deer have home ranges and travel only as far as the need to in order to feed. If the availability of food is a determining factor, I thought it well to find out just where various groups of deer ranged.

It is inevitable that the nimrod concern himself with feeding places, secure areas and the trails that connect them if he is to be successful. If I am being repetitious, it is because I consider this so important.

Feeding is the major activity of deer and other wildlife, for it is the key to survival. Because of that, the hunter should orient himself to such activity if he wants to be successful. Contrary to popular belief, deer do not feed only at night and "bed" during the day. They feed off and on during the day and night. Activity peaks at night and they do feed during the night — but not con- tinuously. They also rest (bed) at night near where they feed. I have watched them stop feeding then lie down or stand while chewing their cuds like contented cows. They can stand so long without moving that they outwear my patience. Normally, they feed heavily just after sunset and again at daybreak as well as during the night. Daytime feeding may be influenced by how much they are harassed by hunters.

Surprisingly, whitetails can be active and be feeding at mid-day, when many hunters head in to camp. As a matter of fact, I have found them feeding at all times of the day. And that demonstrates they do move around during the day if not hounded. But look for them to have favorite daytime hangouts, places they loaf and yes, even lie down. In heavily hunted areas, they are likely to hide during the day and one could well find them bedding in heavy swamps — places they may return to daily. They like to lie down under evergreens, by other trees, bushes or windfalls, in thickets, and, in rugged country, atop bluffs where they have a good view of the surrounding territory.

While deer have regular feeding habits, one must remember that feeding activity can be affected by hunting pressure and it also can be influenced by the weather, for example, rain or severe weather in November. And, when in the rut, bucks may not be inclined to feed much at all because they are busy seeking out does.

The nimrod who still-hunts is likely to find deer feeding, traveling, lying down or standing about in family groups. Don't expect bucks to act like does and fawns. In the case of bucks the hunter could bump into them while they are looking for does or could jump them from their hiding or loafing places. Or he could even find them sparring. In other words, one should expect many kinds of behavior — not just a simple feeding-bedding routine.

In the early fall, deer still can be in bachelor groups. It used to frustrate me to find places where two, three or four bucks hung out and then not see them when firearm season opened in mid-November. In those days, I had yet to learn that the rut could be in full swing by opening day.

Deer will travel farther than normal to feed on farm crops or acorns and they will go much farther to get to a wintering area if they have to. I get the idea, too, that they move more where food is scarce than where it is plentiful and handy. But the beginning

Deer are creatures of habit, traveling the same trail to their feeding area and back to the bedding area.

hunter should keep food and cover in his thoughts when looking for deer. They are associated in good deer country.

While it is true that deer will browse extensively in fall and winter (even eat leaves in summer), they are essentially a grazing animal. Look for them to be feeding in openings, whether natural or created by man, and at the edges of forested land. Farm fields attract deer from spring through fall, for deer will feed where it is most convenient and easy to do so. They can become fond of such crops as corn, alfalfa, clover, buckwheat, soybeans, potatoes and rutabagas — to name some commonly eaten crops. They are likely to abandon all else when the acorn crop falls in wild areas. And, in oak country, they will feed on these nuts as long as they can through the winter.

Look for deer to munch on buds of aspen, maple and yellow birch as well as on "leaves" of such evergreens as cedar, white pine and jack pine. They will invade young orchards to browse on tender shoots and old orchards to eat apples. They seem to consider raspberry briars, seedlings of some trees and some kinds of mosses tasty snacks. Whitetails will eat many kinds of foods, but the state Department of Natural Resources lists these as preferred: Ground hemlock, Northern white cedar, Red Osier dogwood, Alternate leaved dogwood, Wintergreen, Staghorn sumac, Eastern hemlock, Mountain ash, Red maple, Black ash and Juneberry (Shad bush).

What deer consider secure can vary depending on the habitat. Deer in the northern ranges I have hunted use many kinds of cover for security, ranging from northern cedar swamps to farm woodlots. They love dense young aspen (poplar) stands in cutover forests and will hide out in river swales, heavy jack pine cover, brushy uplands, large cornfields, large open, grassy fields or even in tiny pockets of cover in open country that might be bypassed by hunters. Remember, a whitetail over most of its range stands only about 3 feet-plus at the shoulders so it needs and prefers low cover in which to rest and hide.

Learn that deer make trails as they travel and one learns that they are like other animals, including humans — they are creatures of habit. They follow the same routes day by day, and the routes are likely to be the easiest ones they can find that will take them to food and water. These trails could just as well follow an old logging road, a survey line or any route that offers little obstruction. In the various areas I have hunted, deer seem to travel in an elongated oval the definition of which will be affected by the terrain. Where deer are fed they generally have a simple back-and-forth pattern. Find a well-used runway where a buck or bucks have rubbed their antlers and one has the prospects of a productive hunt. If it is a good buck runway — one bucks like to use repeatedly — one will find plenty of rubs along the trail, rubs that date back a few years. A good buck runway will produce bucks year after year. Hunters lucky enough to find such a runway report taking bucks on them annually.

Aside from rubs, deer leave other "calling" cards on their trails — droppings. The hunter should be aware of them, for they can tell a story, too. I don't think much of runways that are devoid of or contain few droppings. And, or for example, a runway devoid of rubbed trees may not be used frequently by bucks. If droppings range from small to tiny, one can assume that does and fawns are the most frequent users of the trail. Does and fawns travel in family groups, while bucks generally remain aloof, often traveling in their own groups prior to the rut and becoming loners during the rut, especially if they are big bucks.

Everyone likes to see deer during a hunt, and I admit to enjoying seeing does and fawns simply because I like deer. But one should not get the idea that if a doe or does use his runway that a lovesick buck necessarily will follow. Buck behavior depends on the season. I have killed only one buck that was close on the heels of a doe, but I could have killed another that was chasing a doe. The one I killed was my first buck. All of the other bucks I have killed in November have been alone.

Early October, before the rut begins, is another story. While bow hunting, I have seen two and three bucks together and I have seen a spikehorn often as a member of a family group, following an old doe and one or two younger deer. Most such spikes have had illegal horns or have not demonstrated any breeding behavior.

The October hunter will run into signs of breeding behavior in good deer country. As such, it helps him determine where to hunt. Runways that show antler rubbing marks are likely to show scrapes, as well. Scrapes are made by pawing and can range from a foot in diameter to close to three feet. The buck will urinate in the scrape and evidently expect a doe to do likewise, for the buck checks out scrapes — even those it didn't make. It will smell the scrape, presumably checking if a doe in heat has urinated in it. The amorous buck will paw down to bare earth and will be more vigorous in making some scrapes than others.

When in earnest in his scraping, the buck will choose a spot under an overhanging branch. Where evergreens are plentiful, an evergreen seems preferred. The scrape is likely to be littered with needles and twigs stripped from the overhanging branch when the buck thrashes it with its antlers and head. I've watched them seemingly chew or at least nuzzle a single branch overhanging a deer trail. Biologists say bucks do this to leave scent on the branch. From what I've seen, I gather a buck will check branches and scrapes made by other bucks. But I also have seen does check scent strips I hung on overhanging branches. In fact, one doe in the 1996 season got so involved that it stood on its hind legs to nose the strip.

Scrapes also are made in feeding areas, maybe in conjunction with making rubs. I have seen a feeding area replete with rubs as well as marked by scrapes. This may well be because does frequent the same area. In fact, feeding areas are logical places for bucks to find the receptive does they seek. While I have been in the woods a lot, I have been lucky enough to see just one young buck mark an area during daylight hours.

The sitter who hunts enough years and whose hunting spans October and November is more likely to see at some time or another a young buck chasing a doe or does. On those occasions it is more fun to watch the antics of the buck than it is to shoot it. Often the buck will grunt as it seeks the doe. Most of the time a

40

wild chase occurs as the doe runs off. My biologist friends say that, frequent as these occurrences are, the doe is most likely to be bred by a larger, more dominant buck.

While I learned something of whitetail behavior as a wildlife management student, I was never inclined to hunt a scrape. Most of the reason relates to the fact that I was a still-hunter by choice. I reasoned I shouldn't bother with them if I had a good buck runway to watch. But I pay attention to scrapes. They mean that bucks are using that area, and, if the scrape is a big one, it could mean big bucks. So if my chosen runway contains good scrapes, all the better. It means I have made a good choice and likely will be a successful hunter.

One must put rubbings and scrapes into proper perspective while remembering that food, security and runways dictate where one should seek to waylay that buck. Ridding one's mind of a clutter of facts keeps hunting simple.

Author (far left) had his first gun at age 9 in this 1931 family photo.

Picking A Watching Place

The late Harvey A. Williams, founder of the Williams Gun Sight Co. of Davison, MI, had a simple approach to deer hunting. "I let the deer come to me," he explained.

Most whitetail hunters try to emulate this approach, but the success rate of deer hunters belies the simplicity of the philosophy. Sitting in wait for a buck can be a sure-fire way to fill your tag, but you can't just pick a spot at random and expect a buck to come by.

The search for a place to watch for a buck starts by learning to recognize good deer country, becoming familiar with the signs deer leave and by understanding deer behavior.

But the best laid plans for waylaying a buck from the sitting position may not help if the sitter is not patient — very patient, patient enough to sit for hours without making movement or noise that would scare a deer. If your bottom gets sore easily and your feet get restless, you may not be cut out to be a sitter.

The sitter obviously begins by looking for good deer cover, places deer like to live in and move through, for that will give a hunter a clue as to where to set up a watching place. It will be difficult for the novice to think like a deer. But even the novice can find deer trails, and, with study, learn where deer feed, where they like to travel and how they react to weather conditions and to hunters.

Although I have killed many deer in the hardwoods, those deer at some time in their daily life spent considerable time in swamps, in heavy evergreens or in thick growths of young aspens. Perhaps because I learned to hunt deer that were associated with swamps, I look for swamps when seeking new hunting territory. I like to hunt tight to a swamp.

However, this chapter (this book, in fact) does not seek to lay down hunting rules, for none guarantees success. Rules are made to be broken and many successful buck hunters can demonstrate how they took a deer by breaking the "rules." For example, swamps seldom figure into farmland deer hunting because there usually are few in such country. But the farmland buck, like northern "deer-country" bucks, seeks and utilizes protective cover. In many cases, a cornfield will do. In others, it's a woodlot, thicket, marsh or swale or even a planted stand of evergreens.

So finding good deer cover, regardless of kind, usually is the first exercise in locating a spot at which to kill your buck. Considerable time should be spent, spring and fall, driving and walking before one settles on a place to hunt.

Protective cover is one-half of the equation in deer hunting. Deer like such places in which to loaf or to bed down and, yes, to hide when not moving about feeding, although the place might not be exactly the same day after day. Still, they can have favorite areas in which to loaf or hide, for one often can expect to jump deer in the same general area time after time.

The other half of the equation is food. Deer spend a major part of their lives seeking food, sometimes traveling considerable distances, depending on the food available. And, as has been said, they make trails as they move about feeding or traveling to and from feeding areas! The fact that they establish habitual feeding routes (not to mention migration routes), gives the sitter something to key on when selecting a spot for a blind. Watching the right trail at the right place and right time is the key to taking a buck by sitting.

So food, cover and deer trails are the basic information a hunter must digest when contemplating a place to sit. Fortunately, choices vary. It can be near the place where deer spend much of their time, near the places they feed or even at some spot in between. The terrain and time of day one expects to kill a buck are likely to influence where one will wait for deer. Or, putting it another way, the animal's routine dictates the watching place. The hope is, of course, that one has selected a buck runway or one bucks will travel when seeking out does.

But deer use trails for reasons other than feeding. Escaping from hunters is one of them. Because this use also can be habitual, the sitter has another opportunity to fill his tag — by cutting off deer that head for cover after being pushed by hunters. I have taken bucks that were flushed out by other hunters, but I have never counted on someone else to help me take a buck. Yet, especially in heavily hunted country, one can be extremely successful by sitting in ambush at the right location.

I met one old-timer who had the patience and fortitude to do this. His camp was in an area filled with deer hunters every season and he did not like to rub elbows with the crowd. Luckily, he had enough deer sense to study the country and find a place where he could sit unmolested and, best of all, see deer.

He had to fight thick brush and slog over ground often muddy, wet or swampy for some distance to get to his "secret" spot. I say "secret" because he would not tell even his buddies how to get to it. One frustrated hunter tried to "buy" the spot from him, but he was not willing to "sell," of course. Good reason. He had found some dry, sparsely timbered ground in that generally wet, brushy country. It was a small oasis of land — just high enough to be dry and open enough to afford shooting. There, he chose to sit against a huge, rotting stump, his feet in a hole he dug between the roots. The hole was big enough to hold a charcoal burner made from a paint pail. Bringing a lunch and carrying warm clothing to put on after reaching his spot, he would spend all day sitting.

He saw little in the early mornings. But between 10 a.m. and 2 p.m., when other hunters — impatient sitters among them — started moving, he would see and kill most of his deer. The key to success was the fact many persons habitually sit from before daylight until mid-morning and then move about or head back to camp. And these same sitters are likely to start back to their stands a couple of hours after lunch. When they move, they can disturb deer. Whitetails are quick to seek heavy cover when hunters tramp the woods.

The old-timer was more than willing to let them drive deer his way, for he had found the place driven deer would filter through as they sought refuge. At the time he showed this deer hunter his setup, he had taken 17 bucks in 17 years from his stump and family members had taken deer there, too.

So knowing or finding out where harassed bucks seek cover can help the sitter find a spot that will pay off. It will because deer are likely to use the same escape routes year after year. By the same token, feeding routes are likely to pay off time after time.

Once one has found what appears to be likely deer country, one can start to look for deer sign. I don't look long if I don't see some kind of sign. Runways are a tip-off, for they can tell whether there are many or few deer in the area. In heavily populated deer country they can be chopped up like cow paths. Where deer are sparse, they may be hardly noticeable. A good sleuth can find them, however, because deer favor walking in certain terrain — along a ridge, for example, or along a swamp.

These deer highways will yield other evidences of deer, tracks and droppings being among the logical ones. Look for fresh tracks and droppings, for they are signs of use. Unless one can find such evidence, it's of little use to spend much time tracing such runways. Look for big tracks and big droppings! They tell you adult deer use the runway. If there is a mixture of large and small droppings, it indicates does and fawns — which isn't all bad because bucks look for does during the rut. It is comforting, however, to find large tracks of deer that travel alone. This can indicate the presence of a buck, for they are likely to be loners during the rut, particularly the older, breeding bucks.

By following well-used deer trails, one can discover other

evidence that indicates whether the area is worth hunting. Prime among the indicators are rubs on trees and brush along the trail. Bucks will rub their antlers on everything from small bushes to fairly large trees and they will rub them often along a trail. They also rub them on random trees in feeding areas. And they can devastate small bushes by thrashing the branches with their antlers.

Oddly enough, some hunters can be oblivious to rubs even in country they hunt all of the time. When visiting one deer camp I began pointing out rubs to a host who seemed surprised at each sighting. Train your eye to look for them and rubs will not be that difficult to identify. Rubbed branches and trees will have bare places on them anywhere from near the ground to a few feet high. Where the bark has been rubbed off, the trunk or branch can be smooth or shredded — as opposed to showing the teeth marks left by porcupines or mice. Look for shreds of bark above or below the bare spot. And look for nicks in surrounding bark caused by points of the antler tines. When snow is on the ground, shreds of bark on top of the snow betray fresh rubs made during the rut.

If there are evergreens along the trail, look at the overhanging branches. It's easy to see places where bucks hook the branches with their antlers, shredding needles and twigs. This likely will occur where bucks paw the ground under the overhanging branch. I figure the more litter there is under such branches the more chance that a big buck is doing the work. The size of the pawed place, or scrape, is another possible indicator of the size of the buck.

Scrapes should be evident along a trail regularly used by a buck or bucks. I like to find both rubs and scrapes on the trail, but I pay more attention to rubs. Scrapes are useful signposts, but they may not be evident if one is scouting deer country early in the fall. But the raw earth in scrapes can be checked for tracks and for evidence of visits by a buck or bucks as well as does. A note of caution if you should contemplate setting up near a scrape: bucks make many scrapes and visit only a few. A good way to check on use is to cover most of the scrape with leaves or pine

This is the kind of rub the author looks for when scouting deer trails.

needles. They will be pawed off if the buck comes back.

I like to find a series of fresh rubs along a trail I am scouting. When I do, I look for older rubs, rubs made the previous year. Such rubs will hardly be healed over, but will be of a darker shade than a fresh rub. Two-year-old rubs will have started to heal. And older rubs will be even better repaired by the tree. A hard rub of years past will leave the tree permanently scarred. Bucks are likely to rub one side of a tree as they walk by it. So the bared side will face the direction from which they come. It helps to know which direction deer are traveling in, for there may be separate morning and evening runways.

If one can find evidence of rubs made over at least a few years, then one can be confident the runway is a good one. That is, it is a runway used by bucks year after year. Killing a buck on such a runway one year doesn't lessen the chance of taking one on it in a succeeding year. Some runways can yield bucks year after year. Finding such a runway is the hope of most sitters I know, for they can then refine their watching place each year or even build a permanent blind.

Once one has found a good runway, the problem is to find the best spot to set up business. I hate to sit on just a single runway. It's more productive to sit where two or three come together. Look for such a place where a narrow thicket crosses more open ground or connects two swamps, where a ridge ends at or splits a swamp, where deer cross a swamp or where there's a saddle between two large ridges, marshes or lakes. Look for natural funnels. Scouting is the key. Scout every bit of the area you intend to hunt.

When one has found a good place to watch, the next task is to determine where to sit. The basic consideration is the prevailing wind. Where I hunt it usually is a westerly wind, coming from the southwest, west or northwest. But it can be in the north and even south during deer season. Betting on the odds, one should figure on sitting east of the place the deer travel through. Where the terrain is hilly or rugged, I like to find a spot that is higher than the deer crossing. Not only is visibility apt to be better, but the deer are not as likely to get a whiff of you when winds cross you up. Remember — passing does and fawns can foul up the works if they smell you! Same thing if they see you, so plan on sitting concealed.

If the sitter is well concealed and can keep from making noise, he need only avoid the whitetail's excellent nose. It helps to bath every night with odorless soap and to wear fresh, clean cloths. If you walk some distance to your blind, dress lightly and carry extra clothing to put on at the blind. Even the cleanest human still gives off an odor that deer seem to detest. Or maybe it just scares hell out of them. The ultimate protection is to be down-wind of the crossing or to be favored by still weather. If it makes you feel better, use one of the new products that supposedly kill or mask scent.

If a spot proves to be a reliable place at which to kill a buck, it makes sense to build a permanent blind there — permanent as in wood. A little shanty will do many things for the sitter. It will end the problem of smell, if you have just one opening to shoot through because the wind will not blow through the blind and carry your scent into the woods. The blind conceals movement. And it can be heated with a small propane burner.

Not only that, one can furnish it with a good seat. With such attending comfort, one can endure hours of watching without fear of spooking a deer by getting up to stretch or move around. If you are like me and can't stand sitting long even in such a blind, take a break. Walk away from the blind in the opposite direction from which deer are expected. Get well away.

I don't advise using blinds on public property, because it opens up too many headaches. But a hunter can build them on his own property, leased property and, with permission, on commercial forest property open to public hunting.

Deer may be suspicious of such a structure, but it will not spook them. Figure on placing a blind a shooting distance away from the deer trail. For a bow blind, this can be 15-20 yards. For rifle, make it 100 yards or more, but at a distance that provides good visibility and shooting. I don't like to get too close because

I don't want to risk letting a buck see me poke my gun out at it. Much will depend on what kind of openings there are to shoot through. But one can always cut "shooting lanes" on hunter-owned land.

There's at least one other consideration when picking a spot for a blind. Think about how easy or tough it will be to drag a buck out. I have passed up great spots because any buck taken would have to be dragged across rivers or swamps. If your legs are old, you will want to be near a road or lumber trail. I have hauled many a buck out of rugged Upper Peninsula country with an all-terrain cycle or four-wheeler. If plenty of young, strong backs are willing helpers, forget struggling with your buck! You deserve a break!

This rough blind is still productive after decades of use in Alcona County.

Still-hunting
The Ultimate Contest

I froze at the sound. The rustle of dry leaves was slight, but distinct — and close. I couldn't pin it to a whitetail or even a red squirrel, but I dared not move because the swamp edge I hugged was well traveled by deer. So I stood, hardly daring to breathe — waiting for a replay.

When it came after seconds seemingly had dragged into minutes, the tension fled like a snapped guitar string. I looked up into the hard maple I was standing by, saw the recalcitrant cluster of dried leaves scrape against a branch as the fickle breeze picked up again and I felt foolish. That was the source of the leafy sound that had stopped me in midstride.

Only when my pent-up breath released involuntarily and the knot in my stomach loosened did I become aware I was as tight as a bow string. I realized I was keyed up, tense as a cougar about to pounce on an unsuspecting doe.

But I had good reason to be cautious, even though the morning hours, when deer are quite active, had long since passed. In the wilds of Delta County where I was hunting, one could come upon a buck at any hour of the day, which meant there was no time for relaxing so long as one was in the woods.

There's no time for relaxing if one still-hunts for whitetails, long my favorite method of taking my annual buck. After giving up the sitting posture more than 30 years ago, I found that still-hunting is more than just a bridge of the gap between the dawn and dusk activity periods of deer, it enables one who has the patience to learn this skill to take a buck at almost any hour of the day.

That cluster of rustling leaves put such a super edge on senses already finely honed that I could almost sense deer. Because I could, I was feeling the runway with each footstep as gingerly as a barefoot boy picks his way across a gravel road. The ridge I was on split a swamp like the hump of a blowing whale separates the sea and each end of this long ridge was hot. As the deer trail swung from the swamp and angled through a scattering of pole-sized aspens, I slowed to a baby-step. I had hardly taken a dozen steps toward the top of the ridge when the head and part of the neck of a nice buck suddenly protruded from behind one of the trees farther up the rise. As the buck stared at me, I craned my neck around the tree next to me, but I was staring through the scope on my .32 Winchester Special. Putting the cross hairs on the white spot under the buck's chin, I squeezed the trigger.

After I had walked up to the downed buck and made sure it was dead, I looked at my watch. It was 2 p.m., a time when most of our crew were still lounging around the camp stove or perhaps thinking about going out to sit for the evening. Clock-watching is a ritual with me when I'm hunting. I clock every kill and I clock every deer I see while walking. The first deer I see on a ridge is not as important as the next one I see at that spot. If I keep seeing deer at the same hour, I figure I'm on to something — a movement of deer at a particular time and place.

I knew that somewhere in the three square miles of hunting territory I bossed that a buck was likely to move at some time during the day. My territory was a series of swamps separated by ridges, some small and narrow, some round, some long. I cut across swamps, walked their edges wherever ridges intervened, followed old lumber trails and probed little pockets of cover. I could spend much of the day, or all of it, walking and never re-trace my steps. The beauty of that walk is the fact I could expect to see deer at almost any time, particularly in any one of five hot

54

Deer Camp in Delta County accounted for many big bucks.

spots. Deer in that country are likely to move any time they feel like it, but it's obvious they do not move on every ridge at the same time. That's why I clock deer, linking time to their movements across or along ridges. Knowing when deer move is the counterpart of knowing where. Where and when are inseparable.

Putting where and when together enabled me to shoot a buck at almost any hour of the day, and I'll explain how to do that later in this chapter. For the moment, I want to stress the importance of learning deer routines and connecting them to places a deer exposes itself during daylight hours. Each year I find but pay little attention to tremendous runways, complete with rubs and scrapes, because the deer only use those ridge crossings at night. I concentrate on where deer travel or loaf during daylight hours.

One of my hunting friends complained one recent year that he had spent 16 days (all season) in his blind and hadn't seen a buck. He was very bitter toward the Department of Natural Resources. I told him he was at fault for clinging to an unproductive deer stand. Sitting and hoping for a buck is not the same as sitting and expecting a buck.

By knowing where and when deer are apt to show up, I can walk my ridges and swamp edges at the most favorable times. I start my mornings walking ridges where I have seen deer in the morning and move on in the afternoon to walk ridges where I see deer in the afternoon. Sooner or later, that routine puts me in front of a buck some time during the day somewhere in territory I claim as mine. It's a system that worked wonders for the 17 years I hunted out of one Upper Peninsula deer camp.

That 2 p.m. buck I shot was taken on a ridge that deer crossed between 9:30 a.m. and 2 p.m. Although I killed him on the north end, the south end of the ridge was most reliable. Over a period of years, I had downed three other bucks on the south end at midday and a buddy had taken four others at the noon hour. The next ridge over was good both in the morning and in the evening. Two others had produced for me in the evening and another was an afternoon ridge. By hunting five ridges, I had scattered kills all over that area at hours ranging from early morning until dusk. My record shows morning kills at 8:30, 9:30, 10, 10:30, and 11 and afternoon kills at 1, 1:30, 2, 4 and 5:30 — with multiple kills at some of these times and places. Oddly enough, that ridge where bucks crossed at midday was the most reliable spot to see a buck at the appointed time.

Although the kills appear to be random when plotted on a map, they are not. They were made because I had researched that country thoroughly and had learned how to match the hours with the activities of the deer. Experience taught me when I might intercept a deer, whether it was traveling or just loafing about. Most of the bucks seemed bent on finding a doe when I inter-cepted them. When I started my route in the morning, I started where I had seen deer in the morning and then progressed to where I had seen deer at other times of the day.

I hunted the morning (and evening) movements of deer, but I did not have to head out into the woods before daylight like the sitters in camp did. Rather I started hunting only when it was light enough to shoot. Deer do move most at dawn and dusk, but

Rich Peterson displays author's Baraga County trophy.

I learned deer are "up and about" during the day much more than the average hunter thinks they are. Depending on their feeding patterns and rutting behavior, they can move well into the morning hours as well as in midafternoon. And, yes, they do feed at any or all times of the day.

Of course, one must remember that a buck in the rut can be on the prod all day. The beauty of taking the hunt to the deer is the fact one doesn't have to let perhaps just one buck dictate when and where he should hunt. When still-hunting, one generally can learn where two or three bucks hang out.

If still-hunting is so productive, why do only a comparatively few take it up? I have learned over the years that a good many hunters do not have any confidence that they can get around in the woods without getting lost. They are ill at ease. I have known some runway sitters who had to be led to their spots. Others were taught, like I was, to sit on runways and they are content to hunt that way, lulled by the fact a runway is at least evidence a deer might come along. Still others find sitting the easy way to hunt. Many just can't still-hunt, try as they might.

With patience, though, most can learn to still-hunt. The first thing to remember is to forget about fooling that vacuum-cleaner nose one's quarry possesses, and the same goes for his antenna-like ears. But the hunter might just be able to confuse a whitetail's perceptive radar system. When I have to make noise, I do it deliberately. I don't try to sneak along, but, rather, I change pace, trying to make my two human steps sound like four hooves of a deer. It isn't easy, but one can break step, pause often and do a passable job of sounding unlike a human.

Don't expect to be highly successful at this game where deer are kept on the go by heavy hunting pressure. It works best when deer are able to pursue their normal habits with little interruption from hunters. And don't expect to fill your tag unless you are at ease in the woods and know at all times where you are in relation to getting out. That knowledge becomes critical when one downs a buck, in fact it is vital even to making the decision whether to shoot or not to shoot.

58

One aspect of being at ease in the woods is the ability to slip through them with the same facility that a whitetail does, keeping both eyes and ears tuned to what goes on about you. For the trick is to either hear or see a buck before it sees you or at least do so at the same time. My eyes are quick to pick up any movement in the woods, but I am first to admit it is not easy to spot a standing deer. Some advice a buddy gave me long ago helps. First of all, learn to look between the trees and then learn to look for brown. The eyes automatically focus on objects, which reminds one to force himself to look between trees rather than at them. If one concentrates on looking just for white, it might be the wrong end of a deer going away from him. I think I depend on my ears a fraction more than my eyes, for they often alert me to an oncoming buck, giving me the upper hand immediately.

It put me on the alert one time when I was following an old logging road across a swamp to get to a little round ridge that was completely surrounded by swamp. I was being particularly careful because I know deer like to follow old lumber trails, too! As a result, I heard the footsteps of a deer in the deep leaves on the ridge, the sound of a deer heading directly for the trail I was on. All I had to do was stop and wait. Presently, I saw the four-pointer coming toward me. By the time it got to an opening I already knew just how I was going to down that buck.

I said it would take patience to learn how to take a deer at any hour by still-hunting, but these 10 guidelines will get one off to a good start:

1. Select country laced with swamps, because for deer stay in them and walk along them — and the swamp edge makes excellent cover for the hunter.

2. Walk the country enough so that your mind has a blueprint of every trail and every place deer like.

3. Walk from daylight to dark, and be able to walk for miles if that is what is required. I always pack my lunch.

4. Walk where the deer walk. It affords the most quiet walking and puts one in position to kill a buck.

Hunting partner Boyd Williams downed this nice buck near camp in Delta County where the author had great hunting years.

5. Walk flat-footed, making only one noise when your foot goes down, just like a deer. Shift weight only after the leading foot has "felt out" hidden dead branches or other noise makers.

6. Walk ever so slowly and stop, look and listen often.

7. Learn to look between the trees, not at them, and look for parts of deer, brown as well as white.

8. Wear wool clothing that blends into the background. It's the most quiet clothing and most suitable rain or shine. I wear green except for the required patch of hunter orange.

9. Do not swing arms or gun about. I hate even to blow my nose, to adjust my cap or to reach up to push a branch out of the way. Deer don't detect a motionless hunter easily, but I sometimes think they can see one blink!

10. Plan ahead how you are going to get your deer out, keeping in mind the nearest driveable trail you can drag it to no matter where you kill it.

Follow these suggestions and some day you will come face to face with a buck on the trail, quite likely when the sun is high and your buddies are lounging in camp wondering how to get theirs. When you do face that buck, your heart will gallop and a hot surge of electricity will course through your body. You may even find the presence of mind to get your gun up and drop that deer. If that happens, you could well be sold on the fact you can walk up your buck at any hour of the day.

Hour Of The Buck

The deer skirted the end of the cedar swamp with all the stealth of a shadow lengthening in the November afternoon sun. The sneak play almost fooled me as shade from the pines at the end of the swamp helped the buck's act. Or was it a buck?

"Damn," I thought to myself, "I know you're a buck. "The animal's every action said "buck" to me — the way it clung to the edge of the cedars, its walk, the way it carried its head. But the "form" I seemed to see atop its head never took shape against the greenish-black backdrop of the swamp.

I didn't dare move as I watched the deer sneak through the pines along the swamp edge, intent on crossing the hardwood ridge ahead of it. While the shade from the pines into which that ridge disappeared helped the deer, it did little to make me comfortable as I sat on a log with my back to a tree. I had never sat there before; it was my first hunt in that wild country. But I sat there for two reasons; one, because it looked like a good place to waylay a buck, and, two, because I was waiting to join my buddy who was introducing me to this new hunting area.

While every instinct told me I was watching a buck, I was not about to shoot. Thinking a deer is a buck is not the same as proving it by seeing antlers. But I had a comfortable feeling as the buck got closer to the ridge. It was headed straight for my partner, Boyd Williams, a long-time deer hunter and an excellent shot. I just hoped he would hear it, because he was on the opposite side of the ridge expecting to catch a buck coming out of the other swamp that bordered this long, narrow highland. All I could do was sit there with the mental fidgets over the possibility that the buck — yes, I was convinced it was a buck — might sneak across into the other swamp unseen.

Pow! Boyd's 7mm Magnum cracked. One shot. How satisfying the reverberation that bounced through the pines about me. One shot meant a dead buck. I looked at my watch. It was almost 11 o'clock in the morning. That was the hour of the buck on that ridge, the time Boyd expected he would kill a buck if any that morning! I was so curious to see whether he had really shot the deer I had been looking at that I broke a rule of the hunt: Don't go paying social calls to a buddy who is camped on a runway. But we were going to move on anyway, and, besides, my curiosity got the better of me.

Boyd was close, maybe 150 yards away, by agreement. We wanted to stay near each other while he covered his favorite ridge at least until 11 o'clock. If no bucks came by 11 or shortly after, we would resume our walk through the deer country. It was my first season in Michigan's Upper Peninsula and Boyd was going to show me some of the ridges that sliced the four-square-mile area we hunted. The ridges were separated by long, narrow swamps that one could easily cross (once he knew where). Once I learned the area, I developed a route that took me along five separate ridges in an hours-long still-hunt.

So it didn't take me long to get where my partner was dressing out his buck. He confirmed what I had suspected. It was the deer that had sneaked by me. The eight-pointer had a rack as dark as the deer was. No wonder I had trouble seeing it against those dark cedars.

"Why don't you stay here while I go get the wheel," Boyd said after accepting my handshake. "Keep your eyes open, this is a good spot."

I had already figured it must be a good place, for my buddy hunted this ridge so faithfully that it was called "Boyd's Ridge."

64

A typical evening after the hunt in deer camp.

I came to call it "Eleven O'clock Ridge," simply because Boyd was constantly killing bucks around that hour. Even though a buck already had kept his appointed hour on that ridge I was willing to wait for that "wheel." It consisted of a narrow cradle made of pipe into which a whitetail neatly fitted lengthwise. The cradle had raised handles on each end that made it easy for two hunters to wheel a buck out over logs, hummocks and hollows with little effort.

I really thought we had had it for the morning as I listened to the noise of Boyd's No. 11s stirring the thick carpet of maple and beech leaves on the ridge. If I could hear that noise for about 80 yards, I thought, deer must be able to hear it for twice that distance. And the shooting didn't help.

Just as I was tucking away the information on how far a man could be heard in those leaves, I heard footsteps in the leaves sounding along the ridge from the opposite direction. I was almost instantly upset, for no other hunter was supposed to be on "our" ridge. But I usually keep still, even when a hunter approaches. One never knows how trigger happy a stranger might be.

As I turned my head to see who was coming, I was startled to see that it was a buck that matched Boyd's eight-pointer. Luckily, I was leaning against a maple, so the deer didn't notice me. I slipped the rifle to my face, waited for an opening, and downed the buck with a shot to the neck. It collapsed within 20 yards of Boyd's deer. I looked at my watch. It was 11:20! The hour of the buck paid off again!

Boyd's buck was the ninth for him at that spot. I went on in succeeding years to kill three more there before a paper company bought the land, clear-cut all of the ridges and devastated much of the swampland. But Boyd told me recently that he had accounted for 20 bucks on the ridge.

Killing bucks at the same place at midday isn't the traditional way it's supposed to happen. If it were, why was it that most of the hunters in our camp came back in at noon for lunch? They

66

were probably taught the same as I was. One is supposed to get up before daylight, stumble out to his stand in the dark and freeze for a half hour or more before the light of day revealed that all of those stumps he kept eyeing suspiciously really were stumps. Yes, and one repeated the process in the late afternoon, going out to his spot to watch a runway until he could no longer see his sights.

The average deer hunter followed this routine when I was a kid and he still does. He does because "everybody knows" that deer move at daylight and again at dusk. This belief guided my hunting when I was a teenager, and I usually got my buck early in the morning, sometimes when it was still difficult to see the iron sights I used in those days.

So why was this ridge such a good spot at midday? Traveling deer. Who said deer had to be everywhere at daylight? They can't be. The bucks killed on that ridge were returning from feeding grounds about a mile away. They haunted those places because that is where the does and fawns congregated at night. They left those nightly feeding areas at or before daylight. But it took most of the morning to reach the ridge. The deer I killed as a youth were taken close to their feeding grounds in the farm country. They did not have time to travel far before I intercepted them. The deer Boyd was taking obviously were not close to the places they sought does or fed at night. Neither had they reached the places where they intended to spend the better part of the day. But a look at the country near where they were shot told me they must have been almost "home."

After I had roamed that deer country a few years, I determined that the bucks shot on that ridge seemed to filter from some nearby farms southward through a string of swamps — some large, some narrow and long. Together, the swamps provided perfect cover for deer heading for or leaving the farm fields — fields that were cultivated right up to the swamp edge.

Although I found one other place to cut off the deer after they left the croplands, the place Boyd picked was the best. There was no way the deer could get to their destination without expos-

Andre DeJournett was ready when this Baraga County buck made its rounds.

ing themselves if they clung to the runways that eventually left the string of swamps and crossed the end of the ridge to yet another swamp.

Deer establish feeding routines well before deer season opens. In country where hunting pressure is light, they cling pretty well to them during the season unless the weather interferes or they find a different food bonanza. If they are pressured too much by hunters, one should understand, all of the things one learns about them when they are not disturbed may have to be thrown out the window. They still are creatures of habit, but hunters can cause them to change their movements. On the one hand bucks can change their routes and, at the extreme, they can confine their movements to hours of darkness. Some old bucks are loath to leave heavy cover during deer season in any event and some never do until after dark. But the investigative hunter sometimes can learn a buck's changed routine and find out how to waylay his trophy.

About the third day of the season one year, I found one beautiful buck runway that came out of a swamp and followed an old logging trail that paralleled a leg of the swamp before joining a two-track woods road. The two-track crossed the thin strip of swamp just before the swamp petering out on a big ridge.

I had walked that two-track many times and had always seen deer tracks on the road where it crossed the neck of swamp. But I had never seen deer and never checked the small ridge along that narrow swamp. I assumed deer crossed either during the night, very early in the morning or just at dark. No one had killed a buck on that ridge, but I guessed that intercepting a buck might just be a matter of finding the hour it headed out of the swamp for that crossing.

So I checked out the deer trail, replete with rubs and scrapes, that cut out across the small ridge. I could not believe that the buck that made all that sign would still be crossing that rather open ridge in the daylight. Since the deer sign on the road indicated deer followed the swamp edge closely when they crossed the road, I worked my way along the swamp until I found a place that would allow me to watch both the well-traveled deer trail and the swamp edge.

While the swamp edge showed no visible trail, I still pinned my hopes on the fact that a buck would cling close to cover that late in the season. So most of my time was spent watching the edge of the swamp. Sure enough, just at dark a buck materialized from the cedars and began sneaking by me, keeping tight to the swamp. Well, it didn't get by! It was a heavily antlered nine-pointer that weighed well over 200 pounds.

One might call this luck. But I say all the signs of a big buck were present. All I had to do was find the hour it came out of that swamp to make it's nightly rounds. I may have lucked into it the very first night, but it was not luck determining just where and how to intercept the animal.

But daybreak is a good time to waylay a buck simply because bucks are moving then, probably still looking for a receptive doe if the rut is on. I tend to analyze that movement early in the fall as deer that are leaving their nightly feeding grounds (rutting bucks more likely were out romancing), deer heading for the places they intend to spend much of the day loafing, resting or even feeding some more. The movement is more readily identified where deer feed at a particular place. Such deer can be intercepted early if cut off near the feeding area.

I prefer the evening movement because one usually can get situated near a swamp, for example, or a feeding area well before the deer start showing up. I stay away from farm fields at night because I have wasted too many hours hoping to tag a buck at such open feeding areas. The deer would come into the field after dusk, giving me only dark shapes to look at. I've had the same experience awaiting deer in cuttings. My best luck when sitting has been intercepting them well before they reach their destination.

That leaves many hours during the day to consider, many of which could be productive if the hunter studies his territory and learns something of deer movement in it. Deer are creatures of habit and the solution to turning one into supper steak often is found in learning where it travels and when.

They do travel during the day and they do look for feeding does during the day. That is why I have shot bucks at all hours of the day. It is a matter of scouting, finding deer and timing them. I take note of the spots where deer are seen consistently, for example, where they cross a road or where they appear at the back of a field or along a ridge. I time them and then check on following days whether the deer habitually appear at those places at the same times. It may be just a simple matter of where deer prefer to be during the morning or during the afternoon. Where they show up during the day could be linked to where they feel comfortable or to their routines, which may put them on one ridge in the morning, for example, and another in the afternoon.

Before I left that U.P. hunting territory I had discovered other places where deer crossed the ends of ridges in the afternoon — at 1 o'clock and at 2 o'clock. I also found places on those ridges where bucks had rubbed just about every tree in sight or had made huge scrapes under evergreens. And I never was able to see deer at those places no matter how often I watched them at different times of the day. I decided that some crossings just aren't worth watching because the deer use them under cover of darkness. They came at hours one could not feasibly hunt them.

But bucks have routines, pretty regular ones before the rut. Even in the rut, when they seem to be on the go all of the time, they can show up at particular places periodically. Get in the habit of timing deer you see when you scout the woods and you may discover a buck that keeps such civilized hours that you won't have to shiver in the dark waiting to see if he comes by at his appointed hour.

Pocketful Of Deer

The swale along the East Branch of the Au Sable River was narrow. It was comprised largely of tag alders and aspen and, where trees and brush were thin, heavy marsh grass that rose well above one's knees. It was just a pocket of cover and that made it a perfect candidate for a one-man drive. In fact, one person seemingly could intercept any exiting deer.

That's why my Dad and I chose to put on a short drive. Since I already had taken a buck, I played dog and Dad stood at the end of the swale. I chose to make a "silent" drive, since that part of Michigan's Crawford County is heavily hunted and I didn't want anyone horning in on our act. So I only made an occasional squawk on my crow call to let Dad know where I was.

It was in one of the wider, grassy spots in the swale that I learned once more that deer don't always burst out ahead of a driver. After I had gone most of the way through the grass, three does jumped up behind me and exited the swale. Despite the noise I was making, the does had let me pass within 15 yards of them.

No loss, I thought, for we were after bucks. I hadn't gone much farther up the swale when I did jump a small buck, almost stepping on him before he jumped up from the grass and brush. He fooled us, too. In about three leaps he made it across the small stream and disappeared.

Needless to say, I was a little upset. Where I could have killed that four-pointer, my Dad had no chance. Still, I knew we had one more crack at it, for brother Don was due in that night. The next day we could pull a repeat of the drive — with a twist.

The next day I posted Dad at the end of the swale, where driven deer "should" exit, and dropped my brother off on the opposite side of the river. I planned to make some noise this time so he could follow my progress up the swale. Knowing where I was, he could walk about opposite me on the other side of the stream. I thought we had that buck trapped, if, indeed, it did decide to hole up in the swale again.

I saw no does that second day. But, when I got to the spot where I had jumped the buck the previous day, my adrenalin was rising. Almost as I was considering the drive a waste of time the same little buck jumped up from just about the same place. It did exactly as it did the day before, heading immediately for the river.

Just in case my brother wasn't alert, I fired my rifle into the air. Almost before the echo died I heard another shot directly across the river. The little buck had almost run over Don. It ended up as venison as a result!

The day reaffirmed two things for me: don't bet that a driven deer won't cross a stream even in cold, icy weather. Secondly, where deer are pressured by hunters, they look for hiding places, even small ones, and tend to stay in them if not disturbed. I don't know why this little buck came back after being flushed out unless it previously had spent several secure days in that narrow swale.

I have a feeling that it had been staying there undisturbed for a few days, for not many deer hunters would think of driving such a small bit of cover. Although there were jack pines on high ground on the side of the river my brother patrolled, the buck chose to stay in a part of the swale that was bordered on one side by rather open country. Swales on either side of the river were so narrow one person could drive them effectively.

Our family had bounced deer out of such bits of cover before, having learned that even a small pocket can be full of deer. In fact, we had a series of places we thought suitable for driving. One favorite place was a low, somewhat marshy swamp. It was small, round as a silver dollar. It was attached like a blister to a long narrow strip of evergreens that connected two larger cedar swamps. Except for that strip of evergreens, the pothole was surrounded by ground containing only scattered trees and shrubs. The high ground was too open to hide a deer, but deer crossed it.

Driving this place was a two-man job, as was posting the logical end the deer might pop out of. I remember this pothole well for it provided my first embarrassment as a deer hunter. I was only in my second deer season on the particular day my two brothers agreed to drive the swamp while my Dad and I covered off where some sparse aspen connected the pothole to one of the larger swamps. Deer liked to exit the pothole there and travel through the aspens, scattered as they were.

As usual, the drivers made a "silent" drive, whistling now and then to let us know how close they were getting. The whistles got closer and closer and it seemed as though I would see my brothers any moment. But before that happened a spikehorn showed up at the edge of the pothole. It stopped there and stared at me. I raised my rifle and, like the novice I was, debated where to shoot the buck, for it faced me with only the neck visible. (Nowadays, the neck is my favorite target.) An experienced hunter could have shot that buck two or three times.

With two drivers pushing at its heels, the buck didn't hesitate long. It dashed right past me toward the other swamp. I shot two or three times at the bounding buck. After it took two or three jumps it reached a spot where my Dad could see it, but it was in the aspens by that time. He missed, too. It was a lesson I never forgot. Now, if I am waiting for a buck, I have all the possible scenarios worked out in my mind and know just how I am going to shoot a buck depending on what part of the body offers a chance for a fatal shot. And I don't delay.

We usually hunted four or five days after the season opened before thinking about making drives. By the sixth day, we figured, bucks that escaped the hoard of hunters during those prime first two or three days would be holed up. Oddly enough, some of those places of refuge were places hunters usually overlooked because they were small, were in open country or maybe were situated along well-traveled roads. But that is why we chose such cover for making drives.

Not far from where I missed that buck was a similar setup. A small swamp almost detached from a much larger one was shaped like a bulging pocket. A couple of hunters could get "behind" it and drive towards a road that crossed the end of the swamp before it petered out in upland that was covered mostly by cherry trees and scattered shrubs. Deer came out that end because a river split the upland and the swales that bordered it offered refuge.

It was perfect for a small group such as ours. One person could make a stand at the road, cutting off any deer headed for the river. Two could drive the swamp while a fourth walked along the edge to catch any "side-wheelers" dumb enough to head out into open country. Once again, this cover held a little four-pointer that did as it was expected to do. It headed for the road. When it hit the road, brother Dick shot. But at the same instant the deer slipped on the icy truck trail, causing a miss. The buck scrambled to its feet, turned and headed back toward the swamp it was driven from. But my brother quickly racked another shell into the chamber and downed the buck before it got to the thick cover.

Our group never ignored possible hiding spots no matter how open the ground around it, particularly if we found deer tracks indicating the cover was used. It is sometimes difficult to assess the situation when the ground is bare, as it can be early in the season. But, with experience, a hunter can judge the likelihood that a small cover might hold deer. Snow makes it much easier to make the decision whether to drive, but, then, it also tells other hunters where deer are.

Speaking of snow, one timber cutter in the area related a story that helps tell what deer will do. He had wanted to cut a 15-acre stand of jack pines, but decided to wait until deer season ended. About six inches of snow covered the ground by then and the lumberman said there was no sign of any deer going into or coming out of the jack pines. But when he went into the stand, he drove several deer out of it. Obviously, they had holed up there

The "wheel" still is useful in getting a buck back to camp in wild country.

during the season and no hunter thought the small acreage of jacks worth driving.

Deer will seek such cover in heavily hunted areas. And they will stay there until moved. I learned that on a baffling late-season hunt one year, a hunt that made me decide to quit that four-square-mile area, even though I knew every deer trail. It had attracted many more nimrods than I cared to cope with. This was my "home" country, yet I had spent two days hunting a snow-covered area that was tracked to death by deer without seeing a hair.

Finally, on the third day, I was hiking up a hill and met 13 does and fawns coming over the top toward me. I knew right away what the situation was. Those does and fawns were responsible for making all of the tracks I saw, making them at night as they came out to feed. During the day they had found some haven that protected them for at least the first two days I hunted. On that third day, someone had stumbled into their hiding place

77

and pushed them out.

I knew that, if I backtracked those deer — assuming I could sort their tracks out of the maze that covered those hills — I would find some pines or thick aspens on the fringe of that area that hunters had been overlooking. A trail road split the country and hunters usually worked east or west off that road. But they hadn't penetrated far enough west to flush those deer out until that day I bumped into the herd.

I mentioned small swamps and river swales as the kinds of pockets bucks will hide in. But sometimes one will find a long narrow swamp — evergreen cover — bordering a river. One such place our camp members liked to hunt edges a rather wide stream that we figured deer might not cross unless pushed hard. An extensive hardwood ridge split the river swamp from another one, but a long arm of the other swamp poked out into the timber, inviting any deer driven from the river swamp to seek its embrace. To the south, the river swamp fizzled out but, to the north, it widened into a more formidable swamp that also offered refuge. Deer liked to follow the edge of the river swamp and melt into that comfortable large swamp.

The secret in driving such a place, or any other kind of cover, is to know the logical escape routes deer might take. We found they liked to cross the timber or run north toward the larger swamp that spawned the river swamp. The key ingredients of the drive: Only a couple of hunters were needed to beat the brush while several others could cover off on the escape routes.

Just as it is difficult to call ducks into places they don't want to go, it is hard to drive a deer some direction that doesn't fit its idea of an escape route. Deer are stubborn, or maybe single-minded. They have favorite escape routes and will do anything to get to them. One of the things they do is duck back through a line of drivers if an attempt is made to drive them the "wrong" way. Where it is tough to line up enough drivers to push deer directions they don't want to go in, often just one hunter can move deer if he works the cover in the right direction.

78

So driving deer successfully does not depend on gang tactics so much as it does on a knowledge of deer and of the area hunted. Here are some essentials:

1. Analyze deer sign to help you decide whether a drive is called for.

2. Select cover that is small enough to be driven easily.

3. If your group is small and faces a tough choice on where to put the manpower, cut the number of drivers, not the number covering escape routes.

4. Drive in the direction the deer want to go.

5. Post the better shooters, but make sure drivers know how to push deer from the selected cover.

6. Do not pick hunters who have itchy feet to cover off. Let them drive. The posted hunter must stay put while the drive is on and must be still.

7. Remember, sometimes the most unlikely bit of cover is the perfect candidate for a deer drive. If it contains just one buck, you've hit a pocketful of deer — a deer bonanza.

Some Walk, Some Better Sit

We knew we had the big buck hemmed off from the swamp. He would have to head for the river swales, the only other thick cover in the jack pine flats. The two young hunters who told us about the monster joined in with the drive, with one of them covering a crucial crossing place on a county road. The other stood on a second likely trail the buck might use in crossing the road. We thought we had the buck.

My Dad and I and one brother took on the chore of driving the heavy jack pines where the buck was seen, while our new companions stood ready to intercept the buck. It was a short drive. In minutes we were out to the road, puzzled because none of the standers fired a shot.

When we got to the road, we found the two young hunters standing together talking.

"See him?" we asked.

"Didn't see a hair," one of the hunters said.

"Who covered the crossing up by the curve," my Dad asked, wondering why the two hunters were together.

"Well, I was covering it," said one. "But I left when I figured you fellows were probably out to the road!"

We drove up to the crossing place. Fresh deer tracks, big ones, in the road told the story. The big buck had crossed the road right where expected. But the young hunter was not there to do his job.

Rugged Upper Peninsula deer country where buck ratio was high.

Did he lack faith in the crossing? Or did he get restless and decide to join his own hunting partner? We never pursued the subject.

Since that time, I have heard many excuses from hunters who were chosen to make a stand and then didn't wait for the drivers to get to them. "Cold feet." "I got tired of waiting." "I thought you guys had changed your minds when no one showed up." Even, "I thought I would take a little walk!"

The real problem in such cases was simply that the wrong hunter was chosen to do a job. I didn't think much about making wrong or right choices when making assignments on a deer drive until talking to Arthur C. Neumann, a rodmaker friend who had matched scores of trout fishermen to flyrods. There's more to it than selling a rod and a line that match, along with a reel that balances the outfit. I learned that when he took me out on his lawn and had me cast in order to determine what kind of flycaster I was.

Flyrods have different actions, some stiff enough to send the line out quickly, even violently, and some with a slow, parabolic action — the rod "working" from tip to butt — the kind of action that requires a slow, deliberate cast if the rod is to be allowed to do its job.

Since anglers come in different sizes, shapes and temperaments, one shouldn't sell an aggressive fisherman a soft (parabolic) rod, Neumann explained. A guy that beats the stream to a froth has to have a fast-action tip that reacts quickly. He wants power, enough to lay the line out quickly and retrieve it the same way. Waiting for a parabolic action rod to work would completely frustrate him. I hadn't thought of this before, but I did know an angler who attacked the stream as if he were whipping it to death. He was a case in point.

By the same token, a leisurely, more sedate angler who not only is willing to make slow, deliberate casts, but enjoys such casting must have a slow-working rod, so slow that he must wait an appreciable time for the line to work back and forth.

Since I am a fly fisherman who loves to hunt deer, I began to think that both kinds of anglers could well be among the deer hunting crowd — nimrods who wouldn't necessarily betray their degree of aggressiveness or, maybe, timidity when in the woods. One could be a "bear" on the stream and not exhibit it in camp. Yet that temperamental makeup of a hunter influences the way he hunts. Too bad camp members can't be observed fishing. It would help many a hunt.

If every member of a camp hunts as an individual, well and good. But, sooner or later, when bucks make themselves scarce, hunting parties are going to think about driving them out of their hiding places. And that means cooperation. It means, the "drive master" must know his hunters well enough to make the proper assignments for a drive.

Then too, sometimes a sitter can be tipped off to places where bucks are seen by walkers. A sitter will have the patience to watch that spot for the hours needed to determine whether making a stand there will be productive.

In our camp, I divided my partners roughly between sitters

and walkers. But the sitters had to be subdivided. Where some sitters could — and did — spend all day watching a runway, others would sit only in the morning and evening. They would pot around in the woods or go back to camp in the middle of the day. Only a couple of hunters favored walking, still-hunting, from dawn to dusk.

Knowing and taking advantage of the temperament of the hunters in camp can help fill the game pole. Walkers can work together in covering territory and walkers and sitters can cooperate in perhaps laying a trap for a buck. A typical scenario for still-hunters would be hunting a long ridge as a pair — not the usual thing still-hunters do. But on a wide ridge, when one takes one side and the other the opposite edge, one might jump a deer out to the other. Still-hunters also can post a sitter at a crucial spot just in case a buck is flushed and eludes the still-hunter.

Since a knowledgeable still-hunter covers miles of ground in routine fashion, he is likely to learn more about deer and deer movements in an area than the hunter who sits all day. Sometimes he gets a line on a buck that moves through a certain area at a particular time of day. Typically, it's a situation best handled by the sitter. Since the still-hunter rarely has the patience to sit for long, he can let one of the sitters in camp know about the buck. The sitter will have the patience to spend the time needed to intercept the buck, if not one day, then probably the next.

But one must remember that a true sitter, a hunter with the patience to be still for long periods of time, should be picked for such a job. This is even more important when driving deer. Hunters doing the driving want to know that the hunter making a stand will be patient enough to sit the drive out, waiting for his buddies to come by, signaling the drive is over. Otherwise, all the effort and planning put into a drive is wasted.

It makes sense to let the hunters in camp who like to walk do the driving. Hunters who can sit all day or at least much of the day should be posted to intercept any driven deer. But we had one other consideration in making a drive — posting hunters at good escape routes who were good enough shots to hit moving deer. It does no good to rout a buck from its hiding place if the hunter making a stand can't hit it.

It's not easily recognized, but temperament plays a part in one other attribute some deer hunters possess. Some are uncomfortable in the woods, perhaps downright afraid of getting lost. One of our crew confessed that he could not find his way around in the woods. As a result he looked for places that were easy to get to and then sat all day. He killed deer. And he was one who could be relied upon to cover a hot spot for as long as it took to take a buck.

The possibility that some hunters are prone to getting lost should affect conduct of the hunt because hunting time is precious, especially since not every day is going to be a good hunting day. The best precaution is to carry a compass and to learn how roads, trails and streams relate to the area hunted.

I'm one of those hunters who never gets lost, but does get "turned around" occasionally. A river swamp in our area always fascinated me, intrigued me enough to lure me into its clutches one fall. The ground was bare, so I couldn't backtrack. But there was a river on the west and a huge hardwood ridge on the east. No chance of getting lost if you have a compass. Right? But turned around? I still puzzle over this one.

I followed deer trails into and through the swamp, trails that twisted and turned so much that I lost track of my direction. Besides, I knew if I hit the river, I could either follow it or could turn away from it and head for the ridge.

Well, I hit the river. But a strange thing happened. It flowed south, which meant it should be flowing to my left as I faced it. But when I ran into it that day, it was flowing "north." It was flowing to my right, even though I hadn't crossed it. I was confused. So much so that I took out my compass and took the northeasterly direction I needed to follow to get to the big ridge. Crossing the ridge in the same direction would bring me to the road that meandered through the middle of our area from our camp.

I still don't know what happened that day many years ago.

But I did the right thing. I dug out my compass and relied on it to point the way out. But it only got me out because I knew the land. I had made a map of the area, a map covering four square miles and containing pertinent roads — and the river. I was glad I had made the map because nothing is as disturbing as not knowing where you are.

One hunter in my Dad's hunting camp was such a poor woodsman that he had to be taken to the same spot to sit year after year. He never let on that he couldn't find his way around, something his fellow hunters had to learn the hard way by looking for him repeatedly until it was decided to nursemaid him every fall. He probably was actually afraid of the woods.

It's difficult in Michigan to hunt in the absence of roads or rivers. That's why I always scout new territory, learning where the roads are and where they go, as well as paying attention to lakes and streams. Before I venture far into the woods, I have a mental picture of the area I intend to hunt.

It's hard to conceive of a longtime hunter who is fearful of getting lost, but I know some have that concern, while others just can't get around without the aid of some kind of road or trail. It's likely many people fall into this category. One can get an inkling of his buddy's attitude towards roaming the woods if that hunter sticks primarily to the roads.

Others may go just a short distance, on a good path, from camp to sit on a runway. They have just as much fun as the hunter who likes to prowl the country and should not be expected to perform in the woods like the knowledgeable woodsman. In a cooperative hunt, they should be utilized according to their abilities.

We used to rotate cooking duties in camp until a fellow who loved to cook joined us. He was perfectly happy to spend the time needed to cook meals and go out into the woods to sit in between times. He didn't kill many deer, but he was happy. Besides, he was a good euchre partner!

When camp members know and understand each other's predispositions, hunting can be much more productive. This is particularly so in making deer drives or in teaming up to take an elusive buck. It also can save hours of looking for a camp member who gets lost, and some do get turned around, at least. It might be the result of fear or just the fact that the hunter just doesn't have the savvy to get around in the woods. Then there is the guy who forgets his compass!

Hunting can be a great pleasure when one has compatible buddies to share the experience. It is even more pleasurable when one knows each member of the crew well enough not to have false expectations of him. One usually finds that the temperament of the gang varies enough that members can fit needed niches when it comes to the kind of cooperation that makes a great hunting camp.

A Question Of Baiting

Sometimes one of your deer hunting buddies will pull a "dumb" stunt in hopes of killing a deer. And while you are still snickering up your sleeve he will proceed to wipe the smile off your face by shooting a buck. The "crazy" tactic I am thinking of seemed so way out at the time that it had the essence of a smart play.

Actually, I didn't think it dumb when one camp member bought a trailer load of apple pulp from a cider mill and hauled it a few hundred miles up to camp a couple of days before deer season opened.

What didn't make sense was the spot he selected to dump that smelly mess. He took it down the trail road that split our foursquare miles of hunting territory and piled it in a small clearing at the edge of the road. That two-track followed a hardwood ridge for miles, but the clearing — the site of an old deer camp — was only a mile from camp. And it was hardly 25 yards across, being bounded by the trail road on one side and a steep slope leading down into a swamp on the opposite side. Hardwoods bordered three sides of the opening.

I thought it a dumb move. First of all, that odoriferous offering was in an opening, the kind of place bucks avoid in daylight hours during the season. I don't expect bucks to come to bait during the rut. Secondly, it was so close to the road camp members used morning and night that the hunter sitting by the apple pulp could almost shake hands with them as they drove by that stand.

Worst of all, one would have to sit almost on top of the pile to get any shooting. This still-hunter thought deer would be too cagey to fall for such a stunt. But, then, I'll admit us old dogs often find it hard to accept new tricks.

The smile disappeared when the fellow who camped on the pile of pulp was first to get a buck that fall. After that "accident" I was still so skeptical that I risked losing a pile of dough. I did because I was willing to bet $10 against killing a second deer at those ciderless apples when another camp member decided to hunt there. Fortunately, I only thought about betting.

He went down to the same stand the next day and shot another buck. Dropped it almost on the road. A miracle? Now I was willing to double my mythical bet when still another camp member decided to try the same stunt. Taking two bucks from one spot surely was a fluke. No way one could take a third buck there. Not knowing that, the hunter went down the next day. Highly optimistic, if not misguided. Maybe, but he shot a third buck there.

When the camp cook concluded this was an easy way for him to get a buck between meal times, this doubter was ready to bet the farm that one could not possibly take a fourth buck at that spot. Luckily, the bet was never made. That evening the cook shot a nice six-pointer as it approached the clearing — the fourth buck in as many days to be taken at or near the pile of apple pulp!

Things like this just don't happen. Except over bait? That it can happen may be why baiting has become controversial. Baiting has become so widespread in Michigan that the question of baiting is being argued annually. And it has gained national attention.

I have been careful to avoid using the word, "bait," because the expression was not part of my deer hunting vocabulary at the time the apple pulp put so many bucks on the pole. It hadn't been a familiar word for almost 40 years! Neither did anyone in camp

Does are easily attracted to corn. Baiters hope the does will bring in a buck.

think in terms of baiting. Yes, some of the sitters in camp did take a few apples out into the woods to put on their runways. One sitter would drop a cedar tree near his stand to attract deer. No one talked of baiting deer. But I can see now that dropping a trailer load of apple pulp before season fits the description of baiting. It was such a convincing "lesson" in taking deer that some camp members are now confirmed baiters, ignoring any question of sportsmanship.

Somehow, I figured taking that first buck over the pulp pile was pure luck. But, of course, I'm a slow learner. I had been killing deer for about 40 years without so much as using an apple to attract them. Matter of fact, still-hunters have little use for bait of any kind. When one kills deer all over the map at all hours of the day, as I have, baiting hardly fits into such a routine.

Still, even in my youthful years of hunting, when I killed deer by making stands on runways, I did not think of taking a few apples out into the woods. I selected buck runways to watch and I killed my buck usually on the first morning or evening. So in around 40 years of hunting I had been able to take my deer without throwing out even a tidbit on a runway. Little wonder that my first baiting inoculation didn't take! Sitting or walking, I didn't have to resort to such a tactic to kill a buck. Frankly, I didn't think of it!

It was only after leaving that deer camp and taking up with my old duck-hunting buddy, Billy De Journett, that I really learned what it is to bait deer. He knew deer and deer hunting well, but he had turned to baiting. He knew how and where and when to bait. Hunting in Upper Peninsula country where deer were scattered and hard to take either by still-hunting or stump-sitting, he turned to baiting to attract deer. Members of his hunting party also were baiters. And, yes, they killed bucks — every year.

These hunters killed bucks when others who hunted that same wild area without the aid of bait enjoyed only moderate to poor success. Non-baiters had a success rate that probably equaled the state average. The baiters I checked had almost 100 percent success.

Baiting, it was easy to see, made a difference in killing bucks. It makes such a difference that it is common in states where permitted.

At this writing, Michigan allowed baiting of deer even though several other states had banned it. Of 38 states surveyed by the Michigan Chapter of the Wildlife Society in 1988, 25 allowed baiting and 13 banned it. Minnesota and Wisconsin were among the big deer states that allowed baiting. Pennsylvania and New York were among those that didn't.

If one hunts over bait for long, one learns that baiting and hunting from an enclosed blind go together like bacon and eggs. Together, they are a deadly combination. I learned the answer one fall when I tried out hunting near a pile of bait left by another hunter. Deer came to the bait from all directions. And that was the problem. I was sitting in a sheltered spot against a windfall. But I still was exposed to the wind. There was no way that I could fool all of the deer. Some deer always alerted others coming to the bait. I didn't shoot a deer there.

Contrast this with another spot where I put my young son in a borrowed blind that was baited. It was in heavy evergreens and the nature of the topography meant the blind had to be quite close to the bait. No matter. Deer passed within a few feet of the blind as they headed for the bait. They showed no alarm. The little shanty cut off all wind, thwarting those wonderful noses deer possess. The boy shot an eight-point buck that followed a doe into that spot. The two came so close to the blind that he could have reached out and touched them had there been a hole to reach through.

Since I shot a buck over bait about a decade ago, I have hunted with or come in contact with many hunters who bait. In fact baiting is a common tactic among those deer hunters, particularly archery hunters. Those who baited successfully used a technique that rarely failed. They hauled their goodies, sometimes as much as a ton, out into the woods two weeks to a month before deer season opened. And they established permanent, enclosed blinds at their hunting spots. This is such a deadly combination that the results are almost unfair to the deer. In fact one baiter friend admits he does not hunt deer, he shoots them.

Deer are highly susceptible to baiting, particularly in wilderness country where food is always scarce. Finding food is a major occupation of whitetails and they will feed wherever it is easiest to find. That explains crop depredations in areas where farmers intrude on deer country and it is a clue why hunting in and around standing crops pays off in farm country. Place food on or near a runway and deer soon find it. More than that, if one places food in the same spot year after year, one can "train" deer to look for the food there. They not only come back year after year, but they bring other deer with them. Successful baiters put the food out early and put out enough so deer never eat it all up either before season or during season. If deer eat all of the bait and it is not replenished quickly, they tend to abandon the area. But if bait is always handy, they will come from miles to eat it.

In northeastern lower Michigan, an area dominated by private clubs, I have seen new runways established through the uplands when a baiting place was established. The bait was the hub of runways radiating in several directions. Curious, I followed one of these new runways through the hardwoods for a half mile, stopping only when the fence of another property barred the way. The trail came from well within the neighboring club.

I am not sure where baiting gained a foothold, but it seems to be necessary in the club country. Here is where Michigan experienced its first widespread starvation — centering around the Turtle Lake Club, containing thousands of acres of private hunting. The restricted hunting in this and other clubs allowed deer populations to build up well beyond the capacity of the range to support them. Although the Turtle Lake Club and some others practice range management now, the typical club does not produce enough natural food to support its deer. Baiting, then, provides needed food as well as the attraction the club needs to provide hunting.

Baiters use several kinds of agricultural products, corn, carrots and sugar beats being the most popular and probably the most effective. But deer like carrots so well that one can hardly keep up with their appetite. Corn is excellent and sugar beats long-lasting, but Michigan State University researchers have listed carrots as most nutritional. And deer love carrots. Hunters also use cabbages and pumpkins and even rutabagas and potatoes.

Oddly enough, deer come readily to such baits even in country where they have never seen a stalk of corn or a carrot. As long as the bait is there, deer will come to it. There is one exception. In country where oaks predominate, deer will leave bait piles in order to eat acorns. It is easy to detect. As soon as the acorns fall, the bait piles are practically abandoned. Those nuts apparently have what it takes to put deer into good shape for the winter. The reaction to the acorn fall is not unlike the way deer go to the first green grass of spring. They will quit artificial food and devour those first fresh shoots, a food that apparently is much needed by deer thin and weakened by winter. A heavy acorn crop is the only thing I have seen that will reduce the effectiveness of baiting.

Baiting, in Michigan at least, is said to be a million-dollar business. But controversy continues. The controversy stems in part from the conflict that arose among bear hunters — the argument between those who hunt with hounds and those who attract bear by baiting. The two groups engaged in years-long argument over the appropriate way to hunt bear, each defending its methods.

After the fury became hot enough, the state Department of Natural Resources started regulating bear baiting. At the same time, unwilling to outlaw baiting bear, the DNR took the first step toward banning baiting by making it illegal to shoot turkeys over bait. The move did not upset avid turkey hunters because the joy of the spring gobbler hunt is calling in those wary toms.

Baiting deer also raises protests from hunters who see deer lured from their territory to nearby private places that bait and arouses arguments among baiters and non-baiters on public lands. Most controversial are those who put out tons of bait, starting early in the fall.

The issue of baiting deer may only get hotter on state land where baiters erect blinds to hunt from. The state has ruled that whoever gets to the blind first can occupy it. Where hunters with guns in their hands argue over a blind, the situation can become explosive.

The ethics of baiting continues to fuel arguments. But those who bait bear will insist that it would be difficult to manage bear through hunting if baiting were banned. Archers likely would be upset if they couldn't bait. The use of bait for them does two things — it gets deer within a comfortable range and it makes them stop, enabling a more sure killing shot. I haven't found anyone who will argue against creating a situation where an archer can make a fatal shot, but I can't say baiting is crucial to making it happen.

Firearm deer hunters do not have to use bait to kill a deer. Yet baiting will collect deer in country where there are only a few per square mile. It makes hunting such areas plausible and enables a better harvest. And harvest may be the secret word.

Game managers continually talk in terms of harvest, taking surplus animals in order to keep them in balance with their food supply or even to prevent them from becoming nuisances. Black bears fit that category when they invade backyards or even communities in bear country. Deer raise problems with farmers and orchardists as well as motorists when they become too numerous. Keeping such game populations within bounds in a state where civilization has penetrated every corner becomes a major goal of management — the same management that wants to produce enough game to keep hunters happy, to say nothing of those who profit from hunting. And the very first to profit from hunting is the state that sells hunting licenses!

Where deer hunters form clubs and where they own camps on sizable chunks of property, they are likely to attract deer by planting rye, clover or corn. All of those crops attract deer. And I have found that clubs or camps that build permanent blinds at the edge of such croplands kill deer coming to feed. Michigan wildlife biologists I have talked to find little difference between killing deer over artificial bait and taking them over crops planted solely for attracting deer. Using scents to attract deer has caused no controversy, yet. But, if they really do attract deer, why is the use of scents that smell like bait not similar to baiting?

I hold no brief either for or against baiting. It helps hunters where deer are scarce and it helps handicapped hunters or those old enough to find walking the woods a problem. I doubt that it can be called unfair to the deer. A deer killed by a still-hunter is just as dead as a deer killed over bait. But one can argue about the fairness to non-baiters. There is no question that baiting can change deer movements. But deer make trails going to bait. And that ought to be a clue for the non-baiter.

People argue over the ethics of baiting, but I tend to think that the issue revolves around fairness to other hunters. If baiting interferes unduly with other hunters, then I think one has a good argument against it. But I would say that, until baiting is generally accepted as unethical, banning that method of taking deer will not come easily.

Meanwhile, those who like to hunt deer will continue to do so and those who merely like to shoot deer will find ways to reduce them to meat. I have shot deer over bait in both archery and firearms seasons. The venison still tasted good. Baiting may not assure one of killing a deer, but it usually brings in deer. For me, seeing deer sure brightens an otherwise dull day.

Scents and Nonsense

The little buck walked right by the pile of bait a friend of mine had put out to entice a deer close enough for an effective shot with his bow.

Without smelling of the sugar beets or even looking at them, the four-point buck went up to an overhanging branch of an oak tree, chewed on the tip of the branch and squatted over the scrape underneath the branch. Then it dashed off into the woods to chase some nearby does.

This was not just a chance encounter with a buck in the rut doing its thing. The scrape underneath the overhanging branch was made by me that very day. And I had poured a bottle of a commercial so-called sex scent over the raw earth. Just like the book said! And it worked!

This occurred in oak habitat in the private club country in Alcona County. Some years later and 300 miles farther north, in Marquette County in the Upper Peninsula, a young buck with only slightly larger horns — a five pointer — went up to an over-hanging branch near my deer blind and pawed the scrape under-neath the branch.

A couple of things were abnormal in this incident, too. I had nailed the overhanging branch to a yellow birch so that it pointed over a deer trail. It was the only lower limb on that tree. In fact, it was the only maple branch this birch bore! The scent put into the scrape was different, too. It was my own fresh urine!

99

"Everybody knows" human urine scares deer away. Don't they? It must be true, for I read in a deer-hunting book several years ago that one must never urinate at his deer stand. Being a self-taught deer hunter, I never knew this. And I was curious. So I began methodically urinating at every stand I made for hunting deer, whether in archery or rifle season. I kept on killing bucks. Maybe I was doing it wrong!

Then one year I put the urine theory to a real test. My hunting partner had started putting out carrots at his rifle blind while I was still trying to take an archery buck at my tree stand not far away. Since it would be a month or more before he expected to use the area, I decided to see what would happen if I urinated on his bait. After all, I planned on being there only two or three days.

Before getting into my stand in late afternoon, I stopped at my buddy's bait pile (note that he wasn't hunting there) and urinated on the bait. After sitting until dark and not seeing any deer, I walked quietly and slowly up a trail road that passed by my friend's bait. Two deer were feeding on the carrots and bolted when I was almost up to the bait! For two days I could not scare them off the bait.

I thought perhaps those club country deer were just too familiar with humans to care. Or maybe they were just dumb. So I decided to try the stunt on some bait I put out in the northwoods where deer were not fed the year around and encountered few humans. I couldn't keep the deer from eating my frugal offerings. Even though I walked into the bait and urinated in it, the deer kept coming. In fact I killed a buck that came to the bait and at least smelled it before being tagged.

I concluded that human urine does not scare deer away. But there's another possibility. Maybe it attracts deer! It will take me a few more years to decide that. Remember, I have only been testing bait and scents for a few of the 60 years I have been killing bucks.

I got started trying out scents when Bob Eastman, who distributes them, gave me some to try. Of course, articles on how

100

great they are were being written at that time as fast as outdoor magazines could print them. The gist of these stories was that bucks could not resist the aroma these scents gave off. The reader got the idea using scents was almost too deadly to be allowed. Following the directions on my free bottles, I started sprinkling a few drops on the deer trails I hunted both in archery season in the early fall and in rifle season later when snow usually fell before my hunt ended. No apparent luck.

I complained to my supplier and learned that he didn't follow the directions on the scent bottles. He poured scent out a bottle at a time! (That made sense because does certainly release more than a few drops at a time.) Armed with that information I again tried scents during my annual archery hunt with a trio of friends. All of us put out some kind of bait, corn, apples, carrots or sugar beets — usually well before season. This particular fall, two of us arrived in camp a day before the "official" start of our hunt. So we decided to go out to our blinds (he hunted from a tree and I was in a ground blind) that night and just watch. We would get serious when our two buddies arrived the next day.

So I fixed up my blind, even strung up my bow to get it ready for the next day. Then I sat quietly to watch for deer. About dusk a four-point buck walked up to the bait where I had poured out the scent. Shortly afterward, it was joined by a six-pointer. Then a spikehorn came in. All three stood around or nipped at the bait occasionally. Then they walked away as if at a given signal.

Needless to say, I was pleased. This was going to be a great bow hunt. The bait worked. The scent worked. I would have a choice of three bucks. Well, not really. I never saw any of those bucks again during the three days we hunted! Does and fawns, yes. But no bucks. No bucks came back even though I poured out more scent.

I decided that perhaps it wasn't enough just to scatter drops of scent around on the ground. Maybe I should make some artificial scrapes near or at my stand. So I chose a spot within shooting distance on a deer trail, made a scrape and poured out the scent. No luck. In fact over the last several years I have made several such scrapes on deer trails with no apparent reaction from a buck.

I killed one buck in the U. P. that I identified as being in the rut. It not only ignored the artificial scent, but snubbed some bait, too. I noticed that deer had found the bait and chewed on it, so I was confident of seeing deer. Oddly enough, in five days of hunting I only saw deer twice.

On the first day of the season, the small buck I eventually killed walked by the scent and bait without hesitating. A short time later, it chased some does back by me. I watched them all disappear. Then I didn't see any deer for three days, even though they seemed to come to the bait at night. I replenished the scent that I had placed in the deer trail near the bait. On the last morning of my hunt the little buck came by once more. But it seemed to have no interest in the bait or the scent. I gave up looking for a bigger buck and downed it.

One year, I got the idea of putting scent in a natural scrape and then watching to see what happened. A buck did come to the scrape at night and paw it after I placed the scent in it. But I had no luck seeing that deer. The scrape was on a logging trail and the country probably too open for it to visit during daylight hours. But, did I cause the buck to return or was it coming back because this was one of its major scrapes? There were signs of does visiting it, so they probably were the real reason the buck came back to check the scrape.

While I was fooling around with scrapes and scents I didn't know that one of Michigan's top deer researchers, John J. Ozoga II, was experimenting with scrapes and scents, too. He made mock scrapes under artificial limbs nailed to trees in a square-mile deer enclosure and compared scrapes where scent was used with unscented scrapes. He and I visit over the phone and I used to stop in his office at Shingleton when on my way to deer camp. He's retired now. John said he found the scents made little difference. The branch and its placement seemed more important.

He told me that the overhanging limb appeared to be the most attractive feature. But he said it must be in the right position over the scrape. The ones that I found to work best were tipped downward over the trail with the tip in the middle of the trail. The tip was between five and six feet off the ground. I pointed my limbs in the direction from which deer came, assuming they would approach the limb, chew or mark it and then utilize the scrape. Still, I put out limbs that didn't work just as I used scents that didn't work.

I concluded that making and scenting mock scrapes may be fun stuff to do, but it really adds nothing to one's hunt if a nimrod has the sense to choose a good buck runway to watch. If one selects a good buck runway, a buck is going to come anyway. How can one prove the use of a scent brought the buck in? And all of this is just nonsense to the still-hunter who walks up his buck.

Of course, I would be the last to say a hunter shouldn't try using scents if that is what interests him. I would point out, however, that one should try one's own urine first. It is about $10 an ounce cheaper and it is always handy.

The All-Purpose Blind

Two brothers already had been introduced to deer hunting before this lad was allowed to pick up his .30-30 rifle — one willed to him by a family friend — and enter his deer-hunting apprenticeship. Until then, he did not realize that deer hunting could be such a religious experience.

Typically, Dad got us up at about 5 a.m., got us fed and then drove into our hunting territory not far from Grayling. He would drop each of us off at a deer crossing or a runway and tell us to wait until we were picked up, usually about 9 or 9:30 a.m.

That very first morning of my first hunt I learned what it is like to make a stand and the memory still is vivid in my mind. It was dark, of course, and I could only barely make out the trees and stumps in the starlight. There was no snow, but the ground was frosty, making walking very noisy. But I was not to walk. I was to sit on a convenient log or stump and watch for deer until Dad came for me.

The first half hour wasn't bad. But then the cold began to settle in — stealing first into my gloved hands and then creeping into my toes. I began to shiver involuntarily. Then I began to pray. I prayed for daylight to come. And, after all of those things that looked like deer in the half-light turned out to be stumps and bushes, I began to pray again. I prayed for Dad to come and get me. Never had I spent so many hours in such a short time in that first wait for deer that never showed up.

Author shoots from a blind that serves both for bow hunting and rifle hunting.

Dad hunted like most others at that time. We went out before daylight to take up stands on various trails or just to watch known road crossings. It was our hope to catch the morning movement of deer. We would cruise around during the day and then go to an evening spot — usually at the edge of a swamp — and wait for deer to come out on their nightly feeding trek.

We did not build fires to keep warm like some posted hunters I had observed. We didn't build blinds, although I noticed some nimrods would throw logs and brush together into a hasty blind and sit fairly well concealed. Some of them would build fires inside the blinds. But we hardly ever hunted the same place enough times to think about building blinds. In fact, as I became more experienced, I never thought about building a blind, because I never killed more than one deer at any one spot. I was not wedded to one place, even though it may have produced a buck for me. Each year I looked for a good buck runway, someplace, and watched it until I tagged a buck. More often than not, that happened the first morning.

No matter, it never changed the routine of sitting morning and evening. It wasn't until my still-hunting years — when I started walking at first light — that I learned the sitter doesn't have to suffer like I did the first several years I hunted. A group of hunters had bought an old farm near our deer camp. They planted all of the farm fields to corn and clover and built little huts about the size of fish shanties — well, they looked more like outhouses — to sit in. Those shacks were strategically placed so the hunters could watch runways coming out of the swamps into the fields.

The wooden blinds kept out the wind, rain and snow and enabled that crew to fill their tags well before our deer pole became heavy. Envious as I was, I thought hunting from shanties was ridiculous and never yearned to hunt in such comfort. But that was before my legs went to heck.

And it was before I quit the deer camp and hooked up with Billy DeJournett, my duck-hunting pal, who understands deer and is my kind of hunter. He was rifle hunting from blinds constructed of plywood. And he showed me the way to the ultimate blind — one that can be used both for bow hunting and rifle hunting.

When Billy introduced me to wooden blinds, I had been hunting deer about 40 years. And I had killed deer with a bow from a ground blind made of brush, from a tree stand and even from a hole in the ground.

In the company of my new hunting partner I not only changed hunting territories, but I was soon to shoot my first buck from the comfort of a weatherproof blind built of plywood, a blind that had closeable windows, a comfortable chair and, yes, a blind that was heated!

I had seen nothing wrong with lying in wait to ambush a buck, but whereas I usually froze doing it, my buddy was doing exactly the same thing from the comfort of a closed, heated blind!

The contrast between sitting on a log out in the woods and waiting in a wooden blind hit home a few years ago when I was hunting some rugged Baraga County country in the Upper Peninsula. I had found a good spot where two or three runways came together at the end of a big ridge. A little swale at the end of the ridge separated it from another ridge that continued in the same direction. Deer either came out of a swamp or off the big ridge and walked through the depression between the ridges as they headed for some evergreens. It looked as if it might be a good spot for a blind, but I had to check it out first. So I decided to open the rifle season under some balsam trees on a little bluff opposite the big ridge and watch the runways.

I attached my bowhunting seat to the trunk of one of the balsams and felt I had a sheltered place to watch from. On the very first morning of hunting season a young buck came by, too small to take so early, I thought. It disappeared into the evergreens and shortly afterward, some does came running out, the little buck in hot pursuit. It chased one almost up into my lap. I had to chuckle. What could be more fun?

The next day I took up my vigil, hoping to see the buck that made those big tracks on the runway I was watching. But not long after I took my seat, it started snowing. It was a soft snow, big flakes floating gently to the ground. There was no wind and temperatures were at the freezing (or thawing) mark. I felt pretty satisfied as I leaned back under the cover of the spreading limbs of the balsams.

But then I discovered what was happening while my eyes were glued to the runways. The balsams were not thick enough to stop much of the snow. I looked down to discover ridges of snow about three inches deep on my lap. I could not keep the snow off my rifle. It piled up on the barrel and it covered the scope. I began to wonder why I was sitting there getting wet. I didn't wonder long. I jumped on my three-wheeler and drove down a logging trail to a driveable road where I had left my pickup. I decided to drive back to my motel and eat lunch there. But all of the time I felt I really should be out in the woods. I knew the snowfall would move deer.

After the snow stopped I went back, walking up the lumber trail this time. It was criss-crossed with fresh deer tracks. Deer seemed to have moved all over in that hour I was absent from my stand. Meanwhile, my son had stayed out in the woods. He was hunting from a borrowed plywood blind, heated no less. During the snowfall, a nice buck came down the runway he was watching. He shot that deer from the dry comfort of his blind. He didn't seem to know deer hunters are akin to duck hunters, that they have to suffer in order to be real — and successful — hunters. Yeah, I used to believe that!

So I went into the blind building business. I built one in sections so light they could be easily carried out into the woods. With help, I took the sections as far back into that rugged U.P. country as we could drive and walk. It took an hour to drive seven miles with a four-by-four truck and another hour to get back to the ridge I wanted to hunt. But we made it. It was so far back that, when a timber company closed off the road, I left the blind in the woods.

But that blind enabled me to put a nice, 10-point head on the wall of my family room. I watched the buck sneak along the edge of the swamp I was watching, seemingly oblivious of the blind. But then it stopped and looked straight at me. I poked my rifle out the window and shot.

My second blind was built to be hunted out of with a bow as well as a rifle. It's much more modest than the blinds my buddy has built, but, for the average hunter, I think it's the ultimate blind.

It measures six feet by almost four feet and has a roof that slopes from eight feet high down to seven feet high. The ends are built only 44 inches wide to permit the plywood roof to overhang two inches on each side. On one end is a hole, covered by a door when not in use, that one can shoot out of with either a bow or rifle. The sides have smaller openings, each closeable, that are used for viewing or shooting with a rifle.

The entrance door, about 22 inches wide, is in the high end. There is room for a small heater, a chair and for hanging clothes and storing a lunch and gear. The blind is on skids so it can be towed by an all-terrain vehicle or by a couple of muscle men.

It requires five sheets of ultra-thin plywood or tempered Masonite for the walls. (Check the discount stores.) These are nailed to two-by-two framing at top and bottom and edges. One of the sheets is cut in half, the halves completing the six-foot sides. The half sheets can be joined to the others by one-by-twos or by two-by-twos. The blind is painted with flat, camouflage paint, the kind I used to paint my duck boat with.

Window framing — for either the sides or the tops and bottoms of the windows — extends all the way between two-by-twos, adding needed wall strength.

The floor is built of scrap 3/4-inch plywood, braced underneath so it is sturdy. Nail it to either two-by-fours or two-by-sixes. The supports run lengthwise and act as skids. The roof is of 1/2-inch plywood covered with roofing felt. Old carpeting on the floor and walls make it quiet inside. The blind is light enough to be manhandled. It is easily moved and positioned.

It is built high at one end to enable a bow hunter to stand up

110

— at the high end — and shoot out the low end. The hole in the low end is cut so one can see out when sitting down, yet shoot with bow when standing up. One needs only a small hole to shoot an arrow through, so I cover the middle of the opening, creating a top hole to shoot out of and a bottom one to look out of while sitting down. The bow is hung against carpeting on the side of the blind. One's rifle also can be leaned against carpeting to avoid noise.

It's a great blind. It is extending my years of deer hunting, I am sure. However, be careful about getting too snug and relaxed in one of these little houses. It is easy to doze off. And one can get an awful jar waking up on the floor!

Bowhunting Up Close

Funny how a person sometimes gets into a sport. I took up bow hunting late in life because I found out I could hit a can with an arrow, a can hanging on a string in an exhibition tent. Hitting the can was exciting enough, but being able to pull the bow without trembling was more gratifying.

I was attending a demonstration of one of the first compound bows, and despite the fact the can was probably only 20 feet or less away, I was pleased to be able to hit it the first try. I had tried target shooting with a recurve bow in 1947 and it was enough to keep me cool toward archery. I shook with the strain of trying pulling that 45-pound bow — shook so much I never thought about archery again until the compound demonstration.

But things change. Over the years, bow hunting became more and more popular and seasons were extended, making it possible to hunt longer with a bow than with a rifle. So bow hunting offered a good excuse to spend more time in the woods. When I found I could pull a 45-pound compound bow easily, I went to the late Fred Bear, who had added compounds to his line of bows. He was still in Grayling at the time and not only steered me to the right equipment, but gave some good advice as well. Still, I probably had the shaky start as a bowhunter as have many others.

I hadn't even had a chance to use that equipment when I went to Rose City to do a story on the late Charles Kohn, who, at that time, had taken 30 deer with a bow in as many years. Arriving in

Rose City, I went to a local restaurant to eat. I found a bunch of bow hunters had placed some tables together and were eating there — and making a lot of noise.

Naturally, they caught my attention. As I looked the crew over, I saw a couple of familiar faces — one of them belonged to Fred Bear. Since he had counseled me only a few weeks previously, I strolled over to the table to say hello. The upshot of that meeting was an invitation to his nearby camp to hunt.

I got to camp the next day in time to visit before hunting. I had no need to ask where to go, for Fred had built a small brush blind beside a trail road and showed me how to get there. I don't think Fred realized that this would be my first hunt. I had only practiced for a few weeks, but I was able to hit a paper picnic plate at 20 yards. "Don't shoot at a deer more than 20 yards away," Fred had told me. I still don't, even though I am a much better shot now.

I checked the place Fred set up for me and found a deer trail crossing the road. It was 20 yards from my blind. So I hunkered down and waited. It wasn't long before a beautiful buck appeared on the road. One problem. It came out about 30 yards away. So I just looked at that hefty, high rack. Then the buck turned and walked up the road toward me. When it got to my 20-yard mark, I drew the bow and waited for an opening. But the buck saw me, whirled and dashed into the woods.

I rehashed that event over and over with myself, wondering if I screwed up. The buck first appeared broadside, offering a standing shot. But I declined that 30-yard shot. Then the buck presented a neck shot when it walked my way. I had been warned about taking such a shot, so I held fire waiting for a better angle. It never came before the buck discovered me.

I didn't kill a deer that first year, but I am still thankful I didn't shoot at the buck. I was consoled by the fact that someone else, more experienced than I, might get to shoot that trophy. Since then, I have allowed several bucks to pass unharmed because they were more than 20 yards away or because they did not offer the kind of shot I now insist on. I want a broadside shot, enabling

114

me to place the arrow just behind the front leg in the heart region.

I hunted from other brush blinds that first year and graduated to tree stands the second year. My tutor that year was Mike King, of Escanaba, a former state champion archer and the most successful bow hunter I knew at the time. Mike liked to place his homemade tree stand among the branches of an evergreen tree because of the cover it provides, and I still prefer such a setup for a tree stand. And something else. He would place a half dozen apples in the runway to induce the deer to stop. But he had a twist, he stuck some evergreen branches into the ground next to the apples.

"When the deer puts its head down to smell or chew on the apples," he said. "The branches will prevent the deer from seeing you pull your bow."

Mike forgot to tell me about squeaky arrow rests. I did everything he suggested when my deer showed up, but the arrow squeaked as I drew my bow and the whitetail raised its head and looked me square in the eye. I didn't get that deer, either.

Oddly enough I shot my first buck while standing out in the open. I had placed the required apples in a deer trail that crossed an unused woods road, but got impatient and left my blind to see if there were fresh tracks in the deer trail. Before I could get back to my stand and the comfort of cover, a buck showed up in the road on the other side of the bait. I had to stop and try to hide beside a four-inch tree.

The buck didn't even look up the slight incline toward me. Its mind was on the apples. But it faced me as it smelled of the apples, giving no indication it might turn broadside and expose a heart shot. I got impatient. I worried that this deer, too, would see me. So I did a dumb thing. When the deer put its head down, I decided to try to place an arrow between its spine and shoulder blade, slipping it right into the rib cage. But I was not the archer then to try such a precise shot. The arrow went low and somehow clipped both hind legs. The buck kicked its hind feet, sending the arrow flying, and disappeared into the hardwoods.

Two does are unaware of tree-stand hunter who watches a runway from 15 yards away.

After cussing myself for a couple of minutes I walked down to find a good blood trail. Reminded me of the time Bear collected a moose by slicing the femoral artery. I decided to follow the trail because it showed up well on the dry leaves. I hadn't gone far before I almost bumped into the buck. It didn't notice me, so I stopped and watched it go out of sight. As it seemed to be looking for a place to lie down, I waited a few minutes and then took up the trail, trying to keep off to one side. I moved slowly and quietly and almost walked past the buck without seeing it. It was lying under some trees watching me. I kept on walking for about 10 yards, then I turned slowly, drew my bow and put an arrow into its heart area.

The deer bounded up and disappeared so quickly that I wasn't sure I had that animal. But it only went about 50 yards before collapsing. I tagged my first bow-and-arrow buck — and after a crazy sequence of events.

Needless to say, I intensified my target practice, deciding I needed to shoot a much tighter group. Meanwhile, I had become wedded to hunting from a tree stand. Still, when a guest at a club one fall, I shot out of a hole covered by an open-fronted shelter. Charley Kohn like that deal, too. An instinctive shooter, he said he would hold his bow crosswise because of the low ceiling in his blind. I also sat in a friend's wooden rifle blind one time and shot a deer through the open door.

That was about the time I was introduced by Billy De Journett to rifle hunting out of a wooden blind in Baraga County's rugged Craig Lake country. Such a blind was impressive. I no longer got covered with snow or wet with rain. I sat in a comfortable seat and shot through a small window. And I was warm all day. I was impressed, but I learned the real advantage of a wooden blind after converting the rifle blind to one I could use bowhunting.

My bowhunting buddy was shooting out of an enclosed blind long before he lured me down from my tree stand. I don't remember just why I succumbed to his style. I had been doing quite well from a manufactured stand or even from a platform built in one of the trees on his property. I liked the vision one has

117

from a tree stand. And I liked to have the advantage of being able to set up close to a runway. But, then, I didn't like getting wet or getting cold while swaying in a tree like a scared bear cub.

In my closed blind I had a comfortable seat and a small heater to take the chill out in colder weather. I kept dry and didn't have to wear bulky clothing. It was something I appreciated more as the bones got older.

I learned these advantages right away, but the big advantage took time to learn. I found that deer never smelled me, even though I could get closer than I ever dreamed. I could get much closer than the 20 yards Bear recommended. Deer would walk within a few feet — like three or four — of the blind and show no evidence of smelling me.

But I had to learn about wooden blinds by watching my partner and by experiencing the crazy things that can happen when shooting from a blind — such as young deer trying to look into my shooting hole. I had already found that I could kill deer 15 yards from my tree stand. I could be deadly at that range. But my partner placed his blind only about 10 to 12 yards from the runway.

I found out when hunting from one of his blinds that, at 10 yards, the deer almost seemed to be in my lap when they came by. I hardly dared to breathe. I let out a deep breath one time, in anxiety, I guess, and the deer heard me. It was too close. I preferred my 15-yard shot from my blind, a shot I could extend at least five yards. But I learned that deer didn't smell me at 10 yards — or even closer.

These blinds have only a small hole to shoot out of — no other holes or windows to look out of. That takes care of the possibility that a deer would see one draw. But I am convinced the deer do not smell me because no wind blows through the blind. I believe deer test the wind for odors and cannot smell a hunter when the wind does not carry human odor.

There's one drawback to the kind of blind I describe. It must be placed well before the season and left there. Deer get used to seeing it as they go by during the weeks before season. If one

Tents still serve some deer hunters in primitive country.

finds a trail used annually, it is best to put up the blind and leave it there permanently. Because of state law, that means one is forced to stick to private land in this kind of hunting. The tree stand is the next best bet and can be placed for a 15-yard shot, too.

Adhering to my principles means learning patience. And I admit I am not patient enough to be a good bow hunter. If I run out of patience, I leave my blind. Usually, however, I can sit long enough to see deer. And if I cannot get the shot I want, I do not mind letting the deer go by. Seeing them is fun, too. I have learned that if I don't scare a buck it is likely to return in a day or two.

And, of course, there are other bucks around that could come in and present a good shot. The satisfaction is not so much killing a buck as it is making a shot that kills quickly. The last thing I want to do is wound a deer. I did that once, which is once too often. Deer hunting is much more fun if one does not feel the need to bag a buck. It is fun to watch deer, fun to see how they act and fun to be able to let them go by unharmed when the mood strikes.

Bow hunting became more rewarding when Bob Eastman came out with the Tracker string. I have had enough experiences over the years to know that sooner or later one will make a poor shot. And that is when the string saves the day.

I made such a shot some years ago, one that sold me on using the string. I was in a tree stand in Alpena County when a buck with tall forked horns came by. It was angling toward me, but I could make a shot in the vital rib cage area. When I shot the buck took off like others I had shot— like a bullet. I was not worried, for I could see the tracker string paying out in the direction the deer disappeared.

The string followed a trail so faint and narrow that it appeared almost to be a snowshoe rabbit trail. It went through some sparse aspen saplings toward a swamp. And it seemed as though I would never get to the end of the string. But it did end right where my buck finally collapsed.

Curious, I decided to pick up the string and measure it when

120

I got home. I was startled to see the trail almost disappear when I removed the string. Without it, the trail was barely visible. Without it I never would have found that buck, for the animal had traveled 250 yards before it died, leaving no blood trail. That's more than twice as far as any other of my bucks ran.

The arrow penetrated the rib cage just behind the shoulder and traveled diagonally through the deer, coming to a stop inside the ham. Although the buck was full of blood, the high entry hole and lack of an exit hole prevented any blood spillage. The sight of the insides of the deer made me resolve to avoid such angle shots. I now shoot so the arrow exits the opposite side of the rib cage. I've had no long chases since doing that.

I avoid shooting at more than 15-20 yards and I always use a tracking string. I talked two partners into using the strings and the success in getting deer has made hunting far more enjoyable. But it is more than that. I think a deer deserves the kind of respect that calls for such tactics.

Making The Kill

The little buck came out of the Crawford County hills down the little draw leading to the valley — just as I expected. It did not see me standing on the big white pine stump as I raised my rifle and followed it out into the flats. I put the bead just behind and a little above what I considered was its shoulder (actually it was the "elbow" joint) and squeezed the trigger.

The buck kicked its hind legs up so high that they were almost vertical over its shoulders. But it didn't go down. It staggered on toward what was then a game refuge. It was only my second buck and this excited youngster worried about whether the shot was fatal. So a second shot was made. But the buck was angling away and wobbling so much that the bullet hit the ham instead of the rib cage. The buck went down, but from the first shot — not from the second one.

This same — older, but not much wiser — hunter was sitting out in the rain in Menominee County one evening covering a runway coming out of a swamp and crossing a ridge. It was near dark. The buck came, but was going over the ridge toward the swamp instead of coming out as expected. The cross hairs centered on the rib cage just behind and above the "shoulder" and the bullet hit true. The buck threw its hind legs up over its shoulders, dropped back on all fours and went out of sight into the swamp. I was about as nervous over the shot as I was years before because the buck didn't go down and because it was almost dark. It was even darker in the swamp, but, luckily, I chose the

123

right runway to follow and stumbled onto the dead buck just yards into the thick cedars.

I should have learned my lesson by the time I intercepted a huge buck that was walking along the edge of a swamp one evening. But I hadn't. Once again — perhaps because I was again shooting at a moving animal — I picked the biggest target. I shot through the rib cage just behind the shoulder. The big buck didn't falter. Instead, it broke into a run, but — fortunately — turned and headed back in the direction it had come from. This brought it even closer to me and I placed another bullet behind the shoulder on the opposite side of the animal. This time it went down and was dead when it hit the ground. The two bullet holes were three inches apart.

I'm not sure where I got my concept of the "shoulder," perhaps from my father, who always talked of "breaking a deer down" by shooting through the shoulders. It took awhile to realize that I either misunderstood Dad or that he really was referring to a buck's "elbow" — that joint between the humerus and the radius-ulna. The shoulder joint — the joint between the humerus and shoulder blade (scapula) — is well forward of the "elbow."

But the heart was always associated in my mind with that elbow and I wanted to put a bullet into that area. I also was possessed by another concept of shooting a big game animal, gained from stories on hunting that I devoured in my youth. I had read all of the expert big game hunters in my teen years and they almost without exception talked about hitting their quarry "in the boiler room," the heart-lung area. Perhaps it was because my hero in those days was Jack O'Conner, who used to refer to an animal's forward rib cage as its boiler room, that I remembered that phrase and let it dominate my thinking when making a shot.

I was to learn that the "boiler room" of a deer is a big one and that there is a lot of space between the heart and diaphragm of the animal. It didn't take many years of watching deer run after being hit (fatally) in the "boiler room" before I decided I wasn't getting the results I looked for. In my early years it bothered me because I worried about making a bad shot as I saw my buck "run away." I was hitting where I aimed. I was in the "boiler room" but I wasn't hitting the "boiler."

I can't stand to see a shot animal even move after being hit. I still remember shooting rabbits in the head with my single-shot .22 rifle when I was a nine-year-old. It bothered me greatly to see them jump around like chickens did when my grandfather chopped their heads off. I changed to shooting rabbits through the (real) shoulder or behind the shoulder and no longer watched them kick when shot. I wanted to make instant kills. I didn't want to see animals seemingly suffer.

I got clues early on in my deer hunting career on how to make instant kills, but the messages took time to sink in. On two occasions I was faced with only one choice in shooting my buck. The animals were facing me and all I could see was the white spots underneath their chins. I put the bead on those "targets" and squeezed off the shots. Both deer went down in their tracks with broken necks. They did not quiver. I liked that. They didn't suffer.

On one opening day I learned by accident of another spot to place a bullet that will cause deer to collapse. I was hunting in the open hills near Hartwick Pines when two deer almost ran over me. They may have seen me, for they turned just in time. I tried to get my iron sights on the buck as they ran almost straight away. When I shot, the buck turned and ran broadside. I knew I hadn't hit it and tried to get a bullet at least in the front end. At the shot the deer dropped on its nose. This shot not only was in the "boiler room," it shook up the "boiler."

The shot was high and in line with the front leg. It was what I began to refer to as the "high shoulder shot." Actually, though I was shooting in the shoulder area, the bullet never went high enough to hit the shoulder blade. If placed almost halfway up on the deer over the front leg, the bullet seemed to raise hob with the arteries over the heart and with the lungs. Deer dropped when hit. If placed a little high, the bullet will go through the shoulder blade and break the spine. Obviously, such a shot also drops a buck in its tracks.

I had learned what kind of "shoulder" shots dropped deer, but it took a session with Dr. Stephen M. Schmitt, pathologist for the Michigan Department of Natural Resources, to discover what apparently happens when such a shot is made. He has done many necropsies (autopsies) on whitetails and, in cutting up deer, has paid close attention to the positions of the heart and lungs, for example, within the rib cage — particularly in relation to the front leg. X-rays help tell the story.

The shoulder of a whitetail is fairly well defined by the muscle structure and although a hunter can pick out the "elbow" much easier, one can pretty well trace the shoulder when looking at a deer standing broadside.

What is not so apparent is the angle of the humerus and of the shoulder blade. When a deer is standing with head up and the legs straight, the humerus lies at an angle toward the neck. A line traced along the humerus from the point of the elbow would run right up the neck to the jaw.

Looking at that same deer standing broadside, one finds that the shoulder joint (between the humerus and shoulder blade) is almost as far forward as the brisket and it is visible just above the brisket. From that point, the shoulder blade slants backward and reaches to the spine.

The shoulder blade and humerus, then, form a wide V that opens toward the rear of the rib cage. A bullet placed in the "middle" of the V, near its apex is the high "shoulder" shot I had been making. It penetrates the rib cage above the heart and apparently disrupts major blood vessels from the heart as well as destroying lung tissue. This is the kind of shot Schmitt tells Michigan elk hunters to make on those huge animals.

On an animal standing broadside to the hunter, the shot is made by sighting on the front leg and moving the point of aim upward until it is about halfway up on the deer's body. The shoulder and leg muscles will define the spot to center on. Schmitt emphasizes is that this target leaves room for error. A high shot will break the spine and a low one will likely break the humerus or elbow joint and still hit the heart region. Missing to the rear

*The author would try for a neck shot on
both of these deer.*

will still catch the lungs and to the front will catch the shoulder joint.

The shot I had selected in my early years was really too far back to drop a deer instantly. It was in the lungs and near the heart, but missed those huge blood vessels above the heart. Where Schmitt's recommended hit puts the bullet in the area of the fourth rib, my hits were around the sixth or seventh rib. There are nine ribs behind that fourth rib, and the heart spans the fourth and fifth ribs. No wonder I got better results when I changed my impact point.

So the front legs are keys to making a good "boiler-room" hit. Where the rule on a broadside shot is to catch that V in line with the near front leg, the advice when a deer is standing at an angle away from the hunter is to shoot in line with the opposite leg. With experience, one can pretty well determine the position of the shoulder joint — that forward bulge above the brisket — and use that as a guide for a shot, especially when a buck is facing you at an angle.

The hunter must remember that a deer has a big boiler room, with the "boiler" at the front. That means one should zero in behind the shoulder joint, not behind the elbow. Only the archer need be wary of the shoulder blade and should probably hold just above the point of the elbow on a broadside shot.

When a buck faces me, I always choose the neck. There's a lot of target there and a whitetail is rarely too far away for such a shot. When a buck is standing broadside and reasonably close, I also use the neck shot. If the shot is high, the buck still will go down and stay there until a finishing shot is made. With a deer facing away, I also choose the neck, aiming high near the head. On close shots I often have shot a deer behind the ear or in the back of the head. Deadly!

Obviously, when one talks of hitting a specific spot, one assumes that the shooter can hit the target. It behooves every hunter (using rifle or bow) to become familiar with the weapon of choice, to be able to handle it easily and quickly and to be able to hit where one aims.

128

That means practicing during the off season. Shooting at a target just before opening day is not adequate. Practice and more practice is essential. Handle your rifle often, for example, throwing it to your face and looking through the sights. It should come up easily and fall into perfect position for sighting every time.

I used to shoot at a 3-inch bull at 100 yards and be content if the bullet hit the bull. Then I acquired some bright orange round stickers that are 1 1/2 inches across. I am not content until I can hit the orange stickers, which I place in the middle of the white 3-inch bull.

Hitting those stickers at 100 yards is adequate for shooting whitetails when one hunts in wooded territory. I use Winchester's ballistic guide when sighting in. For example, if I want my 7mm Magnum to be right on at 150 yards with a 175-grain bullet, I will be 6 inch high at 50 yards and .9 inch high at 100. The bullet will drop only 2.3 inches at 200 yards. This means I can hold right on the spot I want to hit at whitetail ranges because being an inch off is no big deal.

One must remember that most guns shoot better than the hunter can hold. But careful selection of gun and ammo and lots of practice will let one know just how good one is. To make a clean kill is the primary objective and a combination of using the right gun and load, good shooting and selecting the right place on the deer for one's "target" will result in the satisfaction of making a quick kill.

After The Kill

We were out in the dark doing what I dislike most, dressing a deer by flashlight. But one of my bowhunting buddies had dropped a deer at dark and decided to go into camp and eat before getting help to retrieve it.

Since I can eviscerate a deer without even getting my wrist-watch bloody, I was elected to do the cutting while my two partners held the deer in position — a great help. As the evening air was cool, I was not prepared for what happened when I made the first incision in the belly near the rib cage. It was a small cut, but gas came out with such force I could feel it on my face. And the pungent odor that accompanied the gas reminded me of the days when I frequently slit the bellies of illegally killed does found on public land to determine whether the meat could be saved.

This was back in the 1930s when times were tough and the state Department of Natural Resources retrieved illegally killed deer — usually does and fawns. The idea was to save the meat if possible and distribute it to needy families. If the meat had an odor, it was checked closely to see if it could be eaten. I gathered that the formation of gas was the start of the spoiling process. Many deer that were slightly odoriferous were cooked, and the odor became worse after cooking. If tainted very much, the meat would taste something like the odor emanating from it. I remember entering one house at dinner time and almost reeling backward at the smell of cooking venison.

Maybe I shouldn't have been surprised at the gas coming from my partner's deer, for it had been one of those 60-degree October days and the temperature probably was still in the 50s when we picked up the deer. It was warm enough, I thought, to justify berating my partner for not opening up the deer before heading for camp. It must have been two hours before we went back into the woods to get the young doe. As far as I am concerned that was two hours too long. But the meat had not started to spoil.

When fall temperatures are in the 60s, it won't take long for gas to start forming in the deer's abdominal cavity. That it can happen fast also was demonstrated on a recent hunt when I followed up a fatally wounded buck and almost stepped on the live deer. It staggered to its feet and went about 20 yards farther before dropping again.

I had followed that buck immediately after shooting it, as I always do, with only knife and hatchet in hand. It ran close to 100 yards before dropping. Cussing myself for not taking my bow, I hurried back to the blind, nocked another broadhead and eased down the trail toward where I last saw the buck. I didn't need the second arrow because it was dead when I got to it.

I am guessing that the six-pointer was dead for no more than 20 minutes before I dressed it. Yet a small amount of gas came out of the abdomen. That is unusual, however, for I'm hard-pressed to remember seeing gas form so soon. It impressed on me once more the importance of dressing a deer as soon as possible after the kill.

The old-timers didn't teach me this, but I open my deer from stem to stern and prop the rib cage apart to let the maximum amount of air in and, at the same time, to let body heat escape readily. The old-timers also would have torn their hair if they saw this kid wash out the body cavity. But I think it highly important to remove all blood and bits of flesh that accumulate. So I like to carry water with me in the fall to wash the deer out, finishing by wiping the flesh with paper towels. In the winter I use snow if no water is handy. (My water jug tends to freeze in November!)

132

Some years ago, because of controversy over washing out a deer, I ran the idea by my butcher. Beef cattle are washed down in slaughterhouses, he told me, so it makes sense to wash out a deer. If this isn't done, the blood turns "sour" as it dries on the flesh and creates an odor before one gets his meat home. When a buck is killed — no matter how beautiful it may be — it becomes meat. And it behooves the hunter to take excellent care of the meat. It's expensive!

The first priority in handling a deer, my butcher advised, is to get the meat to cool off as quickly as possible. The next is to wash the deer out, which aids the cooling process. This may not always be possible, but one can wipe it out with any number of things — including moss and clean leaves and ferns. I always carry paper towels, just in case. Washing the meat a few hours after the deer has been dressed is useless, the butcher said. I tried it and found it doesn't help much. The meat already had cooled and blood had dried on the flesh.

There's more than one way to dress a deer and more than one "right" way. It depends on personal preference. Because my buddies are rarely around when I kill a deer, I have settled on a procedure that is quick and efficient for me.

I start by elevating the rear end and first free the genitals from the hide and meat. Then I split the pelvis either with my knife or a small hatchet and push down on each hindquarter to break the pelvis open as far as possible. Once I free the urinary tract and intestine from tissue and hide and pull them up away from the pelvis I move to the other end of the deer.

I elevate the front end and slit the abdomen either from the rib cage down or from the cut I make at the pelvis. The position of the belly determines how I start. I continue the cut through the sternum, best done with a small, sharp hatchet, but possible with a sharp knife. Cutting the sternum allows access to the heart and lungs and makes it easy to reach in and sever the windpipe and esophagus, especially when the ribs are propped open by a short stick. It also facilitates cutting the diaphragm from the rib cage.

Then it is only a matter of pulling the viscera out of the deer, cutting the connective tissue that holds it to the back as the insides are stripped toward the pelvis. The easiest procedure is to let the viscera spill sideways out of the abdominal cavity.

I carry a few plastic storage bags with me to place the heart and liver in. The only care in handling the liver is to be careful not to cut the spleen open when cutting the connective tissue around the liver. I am never happy with the condition of the tenderloins — which lie on either side of the backbone — if the deer is allowed to hang a few days. This is precious meat and looks and eats much better if the loins are removed when the deer is dressed.

The hide protects the rest of the meat, but the tenderloins dry up and turn color from exposure if not removed right away. Take a bag for the tenderloins. The heart and liver can be eaten in camp after being soaked in salt water for a time. The tenderloins can be fried in a sizzling hot pan right away and eaten — at least medium rare, please. They are good barbecued, too.

Get the deer off the ground as soon as possible. I hate to see hunters leave such precious meat lie for long, particularly in the early fall. I want air circulating around my buck. My deer killed in rifle season usually drop in their tracks, but bow-shot deer can run even when shot in the heart. That is one reason I always follow up a deer right away if it does not drop when shot. Getting the animal hung up right away helps the meat cool quickly and helps it drain. Blood collects in the rib cage and in the pelvic area when a deer is left for long on the ground. If I don't expect help in dragging my buck out for a few hours, I use my buck rope to hoist it up a tree as far as I can — which usually means I get it vertical enough to drain.

I've only had to leave one deer for long in warm fall weather. It was my first bow-killed buck. I was hunting in Delta County while on my way to a meeting in Copper Harbor. I found a tree that cast good shade and pulled the buck up into the tree until it was well off the ground (using my pickup). Then I wrapped the deer with cheese cloth to keep any flies from laying eggs on the

134

meat. Between the cool nights and daily shade, I figured the deer would keep the four days I needed. I had washed it out well and couldn't detect a foreign smell when I picked it up for the trip home.

Venison does smell. But so does beef and pork and fish and fowl. When I was outdoor editor for a daily newspaper, many harried housewives called me to ask how to get the "gamy" taste out of a chunk of venison given to them. My answer always was the same. I would reply that I didn't know what they meant by gamy taste. But I would go on to suggest that the deer could smell if it had not been handled properly in the field. If so, the meat could be slightly tainted. And the resulting smell and taste is more than just gamy — although the dictionary suggests that gamy implies wild game that is slightly tainted. The acid test is to cook the meat. Don't be fooled by the natural smell of venison. Venison is different.

That's why the meat is prized by so many hunters. If it weren't so good, there would be no reason to kill a deer.

The best cuts of meat from a deer are no different than those from a beef. Tenderloins are prized the most, followed by chops. Steaks usually are tough unless the deer is aged in the same fashion beef is aged. I usually put unseasoned tenderizing salt on my round steaks. Marinating them will do the trick, but the marinade imparts its taste to the meat. Roasts tend to be dry unless plenty of moisture is used. This doesn't have to be only water. It can be orange juice or wine — any kinds used in roasting beef. Check your recipe book for marinade formulas. Sweet pickle juice or Italian dressing are easy ones.

There are a number of exotic recipes for game, most of which I ignore. I do not believe in changing the taste of venison by masking it with strong marinades or sauces. Venison is very expensive meat, so I am careful to preserve the taste. If I destroyed the meat, I would consider the hunt itself a waste — both of a beautiful animal and of time.

Whitetails Are Gullible

The ridge right next to camp had been logged off, so I wasn't particularly expecting to see deer as I walked across on a tote road. As a result, I was walking fast and was not really looking for deer when I heard the thundering hoofs.

I stopped short and, turning my head toward the sound, saw a nice buck running straight at me. It had come out of a large swamp and was running right up the middle of that open ridge. The buck saw me about the same time I saw it. It stopped, but instead of whirling and running back into the swamp like a sane deer should have, it just stared at me. It stood rock still while I raised my rifle and shot it in the neck!

"What a dummy," I thought as I raised my gun. "This is the wily whitetail that is supposed to be so difficult to hunt?!" None of my hunting party was around so I couldn't come up with a reason why the buck should be running out of a swamp. The usual act is to run into a swamp. The small eight-pointer reminded me of another buck the same size that I had taken not far away at the end of the ridge I had been heading for when the eight-pointer changed my mind.

It was a "hot" ridge and I was approaching the best part of it — the south end, the favorite crossing place of deer in that area. I had made it to the crossing point noiselessly by staying just inside the swamp and walking on moss and any log that pointed in the right direction. Now I had to cross the ridge to hunt back up the other side.

The ground was ankle-deep in maple and birch leaves, making quiet travel impossible. But a faint deer trail on an even more obscure logging road led across the end of the ridge, giving me some relief from the noise. I eased slowly across, taking short, hesitating steps — like a cautious deer might do — and stopped often. But I still made what I thought was unacceptable noise, noise that seemingly would alert any deer within 80 yards.

When the edge of the swamp on the other side of the ridge came into view, I stopped to scan it. The first thing I saw was a buck standing 60 yards away in the same trail I was using. And it was looking right at me. My gun already was cradled in my arms, making it easy to slide it to my face with little apparent motion. As I looked through the scope, what appeared to be spikes blossomed into an eight-point rack.

By the time I discovered that, an eternity seemed to pass. But the buck just stood motionless. When I moved the scope from the rack down to its neck to make my shot, I could see the buck's shoulder muscle tense. I quickly dropped the reticule to the deer's shoulder and shot. It whirled, but it didn't go anywhere.

I thought that deer was dumb, too, for it must have heard me coming. It surely saw me. As I ate lunch beside the downed animal, I tried to reason why the deer let me shoot it. Then I recalled other kills made while still-hunting and realized that confronting deer had become almost commonplace. I couldn't think of any that I had downed while still-hunting that I had not met face to face. And some of those bucks had seen me and only stared while I raised my rifle to fire.

I came to at least one conclusion: Whitetails are gullible despite the fact they have a tremendous nose, great hearing and eyes that may not focus well on stationary objects, but that can catch seemingly slight movements.

I have watched hundreds of deer in and out of hunting season and I know they are cautious and alert to sounds, that they test the air with their noses when bothered, that they can be nervous and spook at almost nothing and that they can detect a hunter in open country almost before he gets into shooting range.

I doubt that I would have been so successful over my long career had I not conceded the whitetail's superior trait, — its sense of smell. Give it a whiff of a hunter and it's gone. And one shouldn't underrate its ears or sight. But this great animal has shortcomings that will do it in if the hunter understands them.

For one thing, its nose is of little use on a windless day. Given the fact I have avoided letting deer wind me, I think I get close to deer in part because they are curious. Even though they can turn tail at an odd sound — like a hammer click — they often want to identify common sounds of the woods, like footsteps in the leaves or clicking branches (one can follow a deer through a thick swamp by the noise it makes snapping off branches). While I have spooked them with the slightest motion, I have only confused them at times by waving my arms at them.

I decided that the buck that stood and watched me come down his trail — and maybe some of the others I have tagged — had been confused or uncertain. I was downwind for one thing. And I am sure the buck let me get that close only because not all of its senses were satisfied that I posed a threat.

I made noise, but not "human" noise because my steps were not the rhythmic cadence of a human. Yes, I was moving when the deer first saw me, but I was moving ever so slowly, arms tight to my body — moving, perhaps, like no hunter that deer had ever seen. Or was he puzzled over seeing a moving tree?!

This buck should have bounded into the swamp at the sight of me, but I think it was trapped for a moment too long by its curiosity and its predisposition to want to identify noises. I have watched does move toward me after spotting me before I could stop moving, stamping their feet at every tentative step forward until convinced that fleeing was the best policy. And I have seen deer interrupt feeding to swing their attention to even another unseen deer and stay alert until it came into sight. They can be distracted by squirrels, raccoons, turkeys, porcupines and grouse and probably some other forest creatures I haven't had a chance to observe in the company of deer.I was crossing a small ridge one fall when I saw two deer ahead of me at the edge of a swamp. Although they were about 200 yards away, I was sure I was looking at a doe and fawn. Still, I rested my gun against a yellow birch tree and looked at them through my scope. My gun seemingly made just a small noise against the loose bark, but it was enough to alert the doe. Instead of bounding into the swamp, however, it made a long half-circle out onto the ridge to get downwind of me. Then it came toward me, fawn trailing behind, until finally satisfied the noise was attached to that most disgusting of smells, the human scent. Only then did the two deer run into the swamp.

Bucks do funny things. One buck will spook when you push off the safety and another will stop when shot at. I still remember one embarrassing moment more than 30 years ago when I first started using a scope on my rifle. I was in a little opening ringed by evergreens when I heard a deer coming, crunching frozen snow at every step. Next thing I knew a big rack of antlers appeared in the evergreens not 25 yards away.

I raised my rifle, deciding to shoot as soon as I saw hair in the scope. When the buck's neck came into view, just a few yards away, I fired. The buck stopped and just stood there, turning its head to stare at me. Only when I racked another shell into the chamber did it whirl and disappear into the evergreens. But it made the mistake of running by my partner who killed the 12-pointer. Seasoned at shooting with a scope sight, he informed me that I probably did not let the deer get into the cross hairs of my scope. Then, too, it may have stopped at the instant I shot, failing to take the fatal step I anticipated.

One other time, when I was sitting in rather open aspen country, a small buck almost ran over me. After it got by, I fired at the running deer and missed it. Instead of speeding up, it stopped. By that time I had another cartridge in the chamber and killed the buck. They do strange things.

I think I've discovered how to almost destroy a deer's sense of danger when confronted by a hunter. The idea was spawned on my first bow hunt when I was sitting in a brush blind one evening. I had placed some sugar beets on the trail in front of me, hoping a deer would stop at the smell or sight of them. But the deer didn't come until too dark to shoot. As I heard a deer munching one of the beets I slowly raised up to see if I could spot it. As soon as my head got above the brush the deer ran off. It was then I realized I had removed my face mask as dusk approached.

The next night was a repeat of the first. The deer came after it was too dark to shoot safely. This time my head net was on. I raised up slowly without making a sound until I could see over the top of the blind. The deer — it was just dark enough not to be able to identify it — kept right on munching. Only when I moved to leave the blind did it run.

Later that weekend, I decided to try another spot where I found a good deer runway. It was midafternoon and I didn't put any goodies on the trail because I was merely curious whether or when I might see anything. The only place to sit was against a tree that was probably too close to the deer trail, but I took the chance that I might not spook any passing deer. This time, I was in full camouflage. It wasn't long before three does came along the trail and stopped right in front of me, not 10 yards distant. I wasn't interested in shooting a doe, so I just watched as they fed. As they did so, one doe turned off the trail and headed straight for me. I swear I could have almost reached out and touched it with my bow before it realized I was something that was out of place. Even then, it did not snort or dash away. It merely hurried off with tail down, the other two deer following after a moment, seemingly unsure why they should be fleeing.

That fall, while rifle hunting, I decided to try wearing a face mask and gloves while I sat one morning covering a runway that came out of a swamp. It was a natural crossing and I had tagged one nice buck while just sitting there one morning taking a breather. As I sat there, a doe came out of the swamp sauntering along with no apparent desire to get anywhere fast. It was the last thing I wanted to see, for I could envision the doe spooking just

141

about the time a buck was near.

But I sat still, smothering the desire to scare the doe away and hoping it would finally feed by me. But the deer took forever to get by, following a swamp edge to my right. Finally, it seemed to have decided to stop and feed within 20-30 yards of me. So, watching my runway, I raised my right arm and waved at the doe. Out of the corner of my eye I could see it merely stared at me. Then I put my rifle on my lap and waved both arms. The doe just stared. Disgusted, I swiveled around toward it and waved both arms vigorously. Only then did the doe snort and take some stiff-legged jumps as it moved off, still uncertain about fleeing.

Those incidents convinced me that my face and hands can alert a deer when it sees them. If I do not cover them, they reflect light and are that much easier for the deer to detect when I move slightly. Uncovered, they probably are the major clue to a deer that it is confronted by a human being. Deer have stopped many times when seeing me, momentarily undecided whether to flee. They usually do after assessing the situation. Only when I was a beginning hunter did deer often walk right by me if I stood still. I think they have learned the danger signals over years of heavy hunter pressure. But if they have, whitetails often ignore them!

I have jumped many a buck that was hiding under a scrub oak, an evergreen or even the top of a downed tree. But I think those maneuvers are more correctly attributed to the animal's instinct for self-preservation rather than its intellect. Certainly, bucks make themselves scarce after hunting season begins and all deer seem to react to hunting pressure.

But even trophy bucks can do odd things. One of the last big bucks I shot at my old hunting camp walked right by me even though I was sitting only about 30 yards away from its trail. The rut generally is in full swing during deer season and I suspect that amorous bucks can have their minds on finding does. If so, it makes them vulnerable to sneaky hunters.

Still, bucks have a great ability to survive, equipped as they are with wonderful senses of smell and hearing and possessing the instincts to do so. I am not convinced that whitetails are as smart as they are reputed to be. But, then, I always pretend they are!

Keying On Deer Behavior

"I never intend to shoot my buck over my bait," a bowhunting friend once told me. "I go back up the deer trail (from the bait) to put up my tree stand. And then I make a mock scrape in the trail and pour scent in the scrape. It works."

Another baiter who uses the attraction of food to help him shoot a buck in the firearm season has a different ploy. He hunts from a blind that enables him to shoot his buck about 150 yards from his bait.

Bait isn't the issue here. Deer behavior is. Both hunters find that big bucks tend to be bait shy and stay in the background as does and fawns come to eat. These rutting bucks are not interested in the food. They are looking for receptive does, but they usually are reluctant to follow the does to the bait.

Knowing something about deer behavior helps these fellows tag their bucks. But there's a lot more to learn about deer than what they do around bait. Since I like to learn everything I can by watching whitetails, I like to check my observations with biologists who are in touch with the daily life of whitetails.

And one of the most helpful biologists is John Ozoga, now retired. He gained wide recognition as a deer expert when he worked at the Cusino Wildlife Research Station at Shingleton, following in the footsteps of Lou Verme. Fortunately, Cusino is on my route to deer camp and a good stopping place to break up my trip from Flint.

145

Convinced that knowing deer behavior can help the deer hunter, I made it a point to glean what I could from Ozoga. I originally asked him how biology figures into the deer hunt, but he pointed out I should be discussing deer behavior. When biologists talk about the life history of deer, biology is one subject, behavior another.

Trouble is, it is too easy to oversimplify matters when trying to explain what deer do or don't do. Hard and fast concepts can easily become unrealistic. Among the examples is the much abused term "bedding area." It is useful to understand bedding (lying down), so Ozoga and I tackled that proposition.

Bedding: Yes, deer do lie down. They lie down to chew their cuds and they lie down to rest, conserve energy and to hide. But bedding has no resemblance to human activity. Remember, deer don't sleep all night. They do not ordinarily bed down in one place, travel out to feed and then return to the same bedding area. How and where they bed down is much influenced by their environment (their home territory), by the time of the year (mid-winter, for example), by their feeding habits and by human activity — such as hunting.

This past winter a few deer took up residence in a couple acres of brush and evergreens in front of my home. I found one bed under a pine tree within a few yards of the county road that runs along my property. There were others and I jumped some deer when walking through the area one day. The deer stayed in that cover during bad weather when not out feeding. My driveway is always criss-crossed by deer tracks.

Yes, hunters can find deer bedding in specific areas, just as they find deer prone to loaf in the same area. But Ozoga points out that this generally occurs when shelter is concentrated in one area. And, when nearby food is also concentrated, such as in a farm field, deer will feed in a defined area.

This was the situation I took advantage of when I was a teenager. I learned that those feeding and bedding areas were connected by deer trails. And that made it simple to waylay the deer as they traveled to and from the feeding area.

146

More typically, I have observed, deer travel about to find food that is scattered over their range. And they bed wherever convenient along their feeding route. Ozoga said deer graze or browse a little and then move on to feed at another spot. "A deer's natural behavior is to move and eat, walk and nibble — not to stop and eat everything at one spot."

In these days of widespread baiting, it is easy to be misled by what deer do if hunting over bait is one's only experience. Put out bait and deer will make trails to it. They will even bed, or lie down, near the bait pile, at least under cover of darkness. Then, too, they will visit more than one bait pile if others are handy.

I used to check out a corn field near our deer camp at night. I usually could see deer standing or lying down near the corn. I found it is common for deer to eat for a half hour or less. And I suspect they lie down afterward to ruminate — chew their cuds. Beds show that they do not all lie down for the same length of time. Or, perhaps, the various conditions of the beds indicate deer lying down periodically during the night, staying down longer on some occasions than others. Of course a ruminating deer also will stand, seemingly forever, while regurgitating what it has eaten to chew it again.

Feeding: While some refer to a deer as a browsing animal, one that eats twigs and leaves of woody plants, whitetails graze like cattle most of the time. Yet they will eat aspen leaves in the summer and desert all other food when acorns fall in the autumn. Ozoga and his colleagues agree that "you can't beat acorns" as food.

But deer eat green stuff because they prefer high energy food, food that puts on more fat. Deer in the northern range will browse on woody shrubs when winter restricts the green food supply, but when the first greens appear in spring, they will seek the exposed green areas. I have seen flocks of deer on exposed hillsides in spring. It is common in the northern two-thirds of the state to see deer feeding along highways in the spring, one of the first places food begins to grow because of exposure to the sun.

Whitetails not only show a preference for those early spring greens, but need the forbs and grasses. Ozoga raised experimental deer on commercial foods, but told me deer will ignore commercial pellets they have eaten all winter in favor of the first greens of spring.

Deer eat a wide variety of vegetation, depending on where they live and on the time of the year. When the deer hunter is on his fall quest, he can expect whitetails to change or add to their menu of foodstuffs. In the fall, especially when the bracken fern dies down, according to Ozoga, a period of nice weather can bring on a flush of green, such as hawkweed and sheep sorrel. These are better for deer than woody stuff, he explained. So check out the food when deer change the location of their hangouts.

Expect deer to change their diet when snow puts the choice foods down several inches. They will paw for acorns if the snow is not too deep, but will readily browse on woody plants and shrubs. They prefer ground hemlock, northern white cedar, red osier dogwood, alternate leaved dogwood, wintergreen, staghorn sumac, eastern hemlock, mountain ash, red maple, black ash, juneberry and will eat a couple dozen other shrubs that will help them survive. But, when desperate, deer also will eat food that does no more good than fill their bellies, so don't judge entirely by what you see.

Where I hunt the northern hardwoods, deer are hard-pressed to find food in winter. As a result, they will frequent fresh cuttings to feed on tops of downed trees and they will haunt newly cleared land to utilize new growths. Usually a hunter will either see deer in the cuttings or find their tracks. Close examination of new shrubs will reveal whether the tops have been nipped off. Food is the key to survival, so I pay close attention to cut-over land and the food it provides.

Food and Sex: The trouble with suggesting what deer do or don't do is the fact there always are exceptions. One of the exceptions is buck activity during the rut. Archers can attest to that. Their season starts well before the rut in Michigan and it is not uncommon for the bow hunter to find bucks in the company of other bucks or to take a buck, a big one, over or near bait. For

148

Typical family deer group includes current and past fawns with adult deer.
(DNR Photo)

example, one of my friends took an 11-pointer over bait placed in a two-track woods road. I wouldn't count on this, but, then, I wouldn't count on taking a buck in deer camp, either. But it can happen!

In the northern deer range, it is not so common to take a dominant breeder over bait during the rut. Smaller bucks, yes, but not the big babies. That's because the breeder has his mind on sex and he is daily involved in searching out does that are in season. That means a lot of traveling. So it doesn't make much sense, Ozoga says, talking about food in relation to a rutting buck. "A buck in rut during December is going to lose 20 percent of his body weight. Lay that to breeding rigors, lack of eating and traveling.

On the other hand, rutting bucks are on the go so much that a hunter is likely to see one at any time of the day. This is particularly true of the still—hunter who roams areas where bucks are looking for does. I capitalized on such rutting behavior year after year. In one 17-year period where I kept track, every buck I shot was alone and on the move — looking for does, I presume.

But I pay attention to does and fawns, making sure I travel country frequented by them, because they do look for food. Wherever does concentrate, Ozoga points out, bucks have to go there.

"If you have concentrations of does and fawns at certain sites and you know where these sites are," he said, "you can pretty much predict the buck is going to go from deer concentration to deer concentration."

Seasonal trends: Deer behavior changes over the course of a year, and the hunter who pays attention to deer sign either knowingly or unknowingly takes advantage of the changes.

Let's start with yarding in winter, a time in northern climes when deer congregate in the best cover they can find to avoid severe cold and conserve their energy. Deep snow will send them into yards, but they seem to flock in midwinter, or at least find heavy cover, even when not restricted by snow.

When spring arrives, the herd scatters. Bred does seek out places to have their fawns and are quite involved with the newborns the rest of the summer. In the fall, bucks are together and does can be seen usually with their new fawns and last year's fawn. These family groups are typical and may be larger. And they may even contain small bucks.

During the summer, Ozoga believes, does, fawns and bucks are petty well distributed. One should recognize that deer of all ages comprise the population. Does range from those with their first fawns to those that may have had several, not to mention does without fawns. Bucks are of various ages, although young ones make up the big share, and they congregate in bachelor groups by the time fall arrives. Where I bowhunt I see mostly

150

groups of spikes and four-pointers, probably because the bigger ones are cropped close. But larger bucks run together in early fall and I have seen from two to four of them at a time. Don't look for it to happen in firearm season.

By September, Ozoga says, deer start to group. I have seen herds at night feeding in farm fields and Ozoga acknowledges food may attract such groups, but he believes part of the grouping is related to the fact deer socialize. They do it big time in some cases, then, for I have counted up to 75 on a single Upper Peninsula farm right in deer season.

"I contend that does are territorial when raising fawns, and that means there is spacing," said Ozoga. "In September is when you see deer grouping. "Supporting contentions that socialization is taking place, he said, is the fact one field may have 100 deer in it in September while a nearby field has none.

Does are driven in September, he said, to find good food. The fawns still are growing and fattening and does are beginning to wean them.

It's important that the deer hunter understands the coming together of deer in the fall. Ozoga finds that related does are very social and occupy a common range in the fall. So the hunter is likely to find family groupings here and there as he scouts the woods. The buck doesn't go from individual deer to individual deer when it is in the rut, it goes from group to group, Ozoga asserted.

Bucks probably undergo the biggest change. In October, for example, the bow hunter could well see bucks together. I have seen bucks of various sizes feeding together on October nights. That's when it is common to see bucks sparring, trying out the skills they need at the onset of the rut.

Bucks are still eating pretty well early in the bow season, Ozoga pointed out. But, by the last week in October — at least in the northern deer country — something happens. "They just ignite," Ozoga said. "You suddenly see scrapes all over. You see rubs and, if you see two bucks together, you may see a pretty severe fight."

According to Ozoga, the most exciting time for archers will be the last week in October and first week in November. By mid-November, scraping is tailing off, he said, and bucks are doing something different. They probably are more on the prod.

Like Ozoga, I have never hunted a specific scrape, although many hunters do. "I guess I wouldn't hunt a scrape, but I would hunt an area that had a lot scrapes," says Ozoga. "A buck makes a lot of scrapes that he doesn't maintain. He probably maintains fewer than half of the ones he makes." I think it is possible that dominant bucks do a lot advertising, both for the benefit of does and other bucks. They might not want to or be able to maintain all of them. Who knows. The important thing is that they make and visit scrapes.

So the deer woods are different for the early archer than for the rifle hunter whose season includes the peak of the rut. And it is well to recognize the difference between buck behavior early in the fall and in mid- or late November.

It's wise to learn deer behavior and fun to speculate why they do what they do. "Hunters can get wrapped up in studying deer and tend to forget they initially started out to kill a deer," Ozoga maintained. "After awhile, he (the hunter) becomes pretty damn interested in the critter and sincerely concerned about it, about understanding it.

"I still think that's the salvation of deer and deer hunting in general. That type of person. He's going to be the one the (DNR deer) manager is going to work with better. The manager won't have to bang and bang on him (keep trying to drill biological facts into him). He already has the basic things (knowledge) and you can expand on that.

"The nonhunter is getting interested in the animal, too. That's pretty important. The more the nonhunter understands deer, the more the nonhunter realizes it is a prey species and (that) you can only have so many. We don't have the natural conditions now where we have enough wolves and cougars to prey on them. And

152

that's where the hunter has to play the role (of predator)."

There's a difference between the four-legged and the two-legged predator, however. I see the two-legged predator as a thinking animal, and he will not seriously deplete populations of an animal he respects. With deer, that respect deepens with understanding. And understanding broadens as one continues to associate with and study deer year after year.

These three summer bucks chose to lie down in field despite nearby cover.

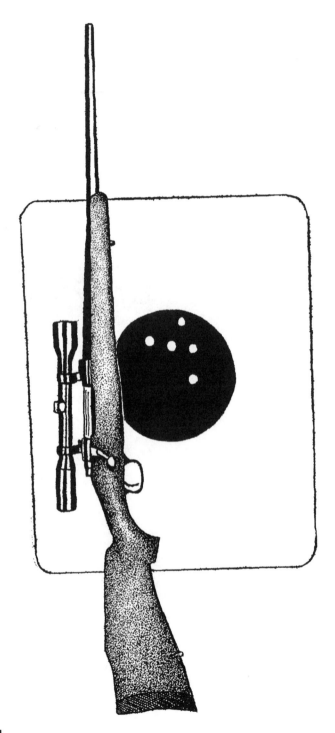

How To Pick YOUR Deer Gun

"If you are going to buy a big gun, why don't you get one with a hole in it?"

Brother Dick's words cut me to the quick. I had just purchased a Winchester Model 70 Featherweight (prior to 1964) chambered for the .257 Roberts cartridge. It shot like a .22 rifle and has since vindicated the recommendation by the late Jack O'Conner that it would be a good gun for my wife and still have all the stuff needed to drop a whitetail.

It turned out that my wife could shoot better groups than I and had no trouble carrying the gun. But, somehow, she seldom got her hands on it after I found out how quickly it dropped deer. But she lucked out, for I went on to shoot several other calibers — pushed by my curiosity over what would make the "ideal" whitetail rifle.

My brother had been willed a .30-06 Savage Sporter in 1937, a gun I have not seen since, and he was happy with it. A Model 45, it was big and somewhat cumbersome, but it did have a hole in the barrel! Roe Clark of Blandford, MA told me the rifle was built from 1928 to 1941. Clark, a former Savage employee, was company historian when we talked. He said 25,000 of the guns were made, the Model 45 being checkered and the Model 40 having plain wood.

Despite its bulky problems, the gun in .30-06 caliber devastated whitetails. No doubt that is why my brother kidded me immediately upon looking over my .257. The bore could almost be confused with that of a .22 rifle.

Author (right) got early insight into deer guns from Jack O'Connor (left).

But I have found that the "ideal deer rifle" is not related so much to the size of the hole in the end of the barrel as it is to the size of the hunter. Other hunter characteristics also come into play when deciding on the "right" deer gun.

Since being kidded about my .257, I have killed whitetails with several calibers ranging up to the .300 H&H Magnum. But studies of gun catalogs told me that I could never test all of the rifles meant for deer and other big game. So, in late years, I depend on two calibers, one for still-hunting, the other for shooting from a blind.

I like my .32 Winchester carbine and my .257 Roberts custom bolt action for still-hunting. They are short and easy to carry through the woods. I can put them to my face quickly for fast shooting. When shooting from a blind, I use my 7mm magnum, another custom-made rifle. When slung, it might drag in the snow in rough country, but it is ideal for shooting from a blind or from a rest in open country.

I am satisfied with what I shoot, but questions persist among beginning deer hunters about what makes an ideal deer gun. That's probably because so many calibers have flooded the market that all kinds of discussion (argument) has been elicited over which is best.

156

So I don't blame the youth who asked me:

"What kind of gun should I get to hunt deer?" The question came after I had finished teaching a session on guns at a hunter safety class for youths and others who were seeking their first Michigan hunting licenses.

"Well, you can kill deer with anything from a .22 (rimfire) rifle to an elephant gun," I advised the inquisitive 12-year-old."

"Sir. It's illegal to hunt deer with a .22 in Michigan," the bright youngster shot back.

But he didn't catch me off guard. I explained that I meant it is possible to kill deer with many kinds of guns, depending on the range and placement of a bullet. I was thinking at the time of a trapper who had a single-shot .22 rifle short enough to fit into his hip boots. It was rumored, if not known, that he killed deer illegally with that gun (by a well-placed bullet to the brain, I assume.) I knew .22 rifles were used regularly on the farm to kill pigs and cattle.

I went through the familiar firearm liturgy with the boy — you know, the well-worn saying that the .30-30 has been called America's favorite deer gun and that the .30-06 rifle has been tagged as possibly the best all-around gun. It's killed everything from deer to elephants. The .30-06 has killed so many deer that one could hardly go wrong buying it. Or could one?

The size of "the hole in the end of the barrel" is just one consideration in buying a deer gun. Whether the buyer is male or female figures into the selection just as does the size of the purchaser — weight and age for example. Personal preferences for actions — bolt action, slide action or automatic (self-loading) — must be considered. Choices also may depend on the level of one's skill in rifle shooting and handling. And one's hunting style also is an important factor. Price weighs heavily in the selections many make.

Suppose the buyer is a 14-year-old beginning deer hunter or a 110-pound woman looking for a first deer gun — like my wife was, for example. It's not likely a slight person of either gender would be happy with the recoil of a .30-06, even when a recoil pad is attached. I certainly would not shoot one without a recoil pad and I weigh 180.

(The .30-06, .300 Winchester and .300 Winchester magnum all are guns that will pound the shooter — not to mention other magnums.) No, the .257 (or similar caliber) would be a much better choice for the youngster and female hunter of slight build and would kill whitetails.

As a matter of fact, the .257 is touted as a fine long-range gun and is rated as adequate for antelope, sheep or goats and black bear. Handloaders can turn it into an even better big-game rifle with proper powder and bullet choice. The whitetail deer hunter seldom gets an opportunity for a long shot. But I did down one small buck in its tracks with my .257, making a neck shot at an estimated 200 yards.

I was using a receiver ("peep") sight and the front bead covered up the whitetail's neck, which was all I could see. As the buck kept disappearing, I raised my rifle several times before realizing the deer had not run but was merely hidden by the front sight. I concluded that, if my bead covered up my target, I must be on. I was! That occasion convinced me I should have a telescope sight. I went the route, open iron sights — good and bad — receiver sights of various kinds and, finally, scope sights. I put them on everything from my .22 to my H&H Magnum. I would never recommend anything but a scope sight now that I have shot deer and other big game at many yardages in country ranging from brush to open mountain landscapes. At closer ranges one merely narrows the target — to the neck or head, for example.

Harvey Williams believed one can shoot only as good as he can see. And I can see to shoot best when looking through a scope sight, whether it is shooting in brush or open country. At Michigan ranges I can count the hairs on a whitetail's head when checking out the antlers. With such vision, I can zero in on any spot where I want to place a bullet.

For a long time my standard scope was a 4-power. My first experience at mountain hunting introduced me to the higher powers needed for long-range shooting. Consequently, I got into variable-power scopes — typically ranging from 3X to 9X. The higher powers are good for longer ranges and low powers good for Michigan deer hunting. I now have several variable scopes. They make it possible to choose the gun and scope combination best suited to the game and/or country being hunted.

Because there are so many calibers — and a range of ballistics — I think one can be misled in selecting a deer gun just by using the ballistics charts, although ballistics is a useful guide.

There are other considerations when selecting a deer rifle. If one is a still-hunter, it means lots of walking — through the brush. For the hunter on the move a short-barreled, lightweight gun is in order. Add a sling and it helps make carrying a rifle so much easier when walking. I have hunted with only one other skilled still-hunter. He is Richard L. Williams, who retired as a partner in the Williams Gun Sight Co. before the company was sold. He used a .30-30 Winchester Model 55 carbine. I used a Winchester .32 Special, Model 94 carbine (the old saddle gun). One could get either gun into action quickly and the guns did the job for the average distances of maybe 60 to 90 yards. I had only one long shot in 17 years of hunting with Dick, killing a small whitetail at 150 paces with my .32. I shot it in the neck, thanks to being able to pick it out in heavy evergreens with the scope sight.

In more open whitetail country, as in the West, one can get shots exceeding 150 yards. But this only emphasizes the fact that the ranges at which one expects to kill a whitetail also figure into determining the best rifle. One should consider a gun with good firepower and a flat trajectory (low rise above line of sight at mid-range) for shooting at longer ranges. The trick is to get one that can be sighted in to hit the mark at the expected range, yet still be in the ballpark at more extreme ranges one might encounter. Here's where ballistics of the cartridges you are considering can be handy.

Another lightweight, short rifle that I like very much is the Savage Model 99. At last check it was available only in two calibers, .243 Winchester and .308 Winchester — both deer killers. This gun is great for the still-hunter. My grandfather had two, chambered for the .300 Savage and .303 Savage. He killed deer for the lumber camps with these guns. One might find these calibers in used guns. Both are comparable to the .30-30 or .32.

Since I have been forced in late years to stick pretty much to shooting from a blind, I have been using a custom-made 7 mm (Remington) magnum. It has more firepower than one needs for whitetails, but I use it because it is very accurate. It has a flat trajectory and kills quickly and cleanly, stopping bucks in their tracks. I still try to do some walking or scouting from time to time just to get away from the boredom of sitting. But this 7mm is not the gun for walking. Since I carry it slung with barrel down, the 7mm's long barrel keeps hitting ferns, low brush — even snow when I walk over rough terrain.

I always carry my gun barrel down in order to get it into action quickly. Using the method taught by Harvey Williams, one can get the gun up fast and still be in the sling. This is a must for the still-hunter.

I imagine thousands upon thousands of deer have been killed with the .30-30. It is adequate for whitetails at ranges they are usually shot at. But there is another reason for considering one. The .30-30 has been called by Richard Williams, the kind of rifle "the farm boy can afford." And that's a good point. My first rifle was a Marlin .30-30 "long tom". It was inexpensive and killed many deer. Affordability is a key factor for many in selecting a deer rifle.

So how about those people who are able to devote little time to gun handling and shooting in the off season? Perhaps an autoloader would be the right choice. All one has to do is pull the trigger. Autoloaders (semi-automatics) come in typical calibers used for deer — the .308 for example. The .308 is about equivalent to the .30-06, when both push the 150-grain bullet.

The only autoloader I killed deer with was the .351 Winchester, a short, clubby rifle that was a poor deer gun because it lacked the punch to put down a whitetail decisively.

But, oddly enough, lots of deer have been killed with cartridges that are less than ideal! By contrast to the .351, the Remington Model 8 autoloader (I shot one in .32 caliber) was very accurate and did a job on whitetails. But it also had a short, heavy barrel and other disadvantages that probably hastened its doom as a deer gun.

I tried a Remington autoloader in .35 caliber at a running deer target. I thought to myself I would get in two shots as the target came by. No such thing. After the first shot I found myself seeing nothing but sky over the barrel. By the time I got the gun horizontal again, the target was gone. The recoil was punishing and also sent the barrel skyward as the gun kicked back.

So, once again, here's another factor that must be considered in selecting a deer gun. One will have to check out an automatic carefully to see if one can shoot it. I will add, however, that I could have killed the biggest buck I have ever seen in deer season had I been carrying an automatic. That's because I goofed on the first shot and the moving buck merely stopped to look at me. I had to rack another cartridge into the chamber of my bolt action rifle (I couldn't do it quickly and smoothly at the time). The buck didn't wait for me to get the gun into action again, disappearing immediately into the evergreens. But that 12-pointer ran by a buddy who didn't miss!

Probably the top recommendation for using an autoloader is that it may be the best gun for the hunter who does not want to spend the time learning to rack a bolt action or lever action or even a slide action fast in order to get off a second shot. It would be a good choice for the left-handed shooter, as would the lever action rifle. The lefty who wants a bolt-action must order one with a left-hand bolt unless, like some, he is content to reach over the receiver and operate the right-handed bolt with his left hand.

Other considerations for picking an autoloader aside, one should heed the advice of Harvey Williams: "The Williams boys kill their deer with the cartridge that's in the chamber!" In other words, the first shot is usually the best, so don't be sloppy in shooting just because you have more shells in the magazine.

Asking what kind a rifle one should buy is a legitimate question — but one that has many answers, answers that are best given when the adviser has some pertinent information about the prospective buyer. Hunters come in many ages, sizes and shapes and weights as well as in both genders. Then there is the simple matter of personal preference in type of action or caliber.

Assuming that deer can be killed with any number of calibers ranging from .25 to .45 caliber, there are at least three dozen calibers of rifles (not to mention handguns and shotguns) that will kill deer. Some of them, of course, also will kill some of the most dangerous game on earth, so one would hardly want to use them on deer. But given the fact there are so many calibers for bolt action, slide action and autoloading rifles that will kill deer, one has a good opportunity to select a rifle that suits the purchaser. One only has to keep in mind recoil, weight, length, price, type of hunting and personal preferences for the type of action.

I have used several kinds of rifles to kill deer, simply because I had the opportunity to try them out. For example, I started with a .30-30 Marlin because the gun was willed to me by an old-timer. It was my first "big bore" and enabled me to start deer hunting at age 15, a year earlier than my Dad had decided his kids were old enough to handle such guns.

I went on to kill many deer with the .32 Winchester Special carbine and the .257 Roberts as well as with the .351 Winchester, the .308 Winchester, .280 Remington, .300 H & H Magnum (yes, really) and 7 mm Mag. And I have dropped deer in their tracks with a .50 caliber muzzleloader.

There are other cartridges in the deer-gun class. They include the .300 Savage, .250 Savage, .270 Winchester, .264 Winchester magnum, .284 Winchester, 7mm Mauser, .44 Remington magnum, .280 Remington and the .444 Marlin — to name some of the more popular. But one is likely to see old-time calibers still being used successfully as well as calibers that are meant for much bigger game.

Once one has decided on the make of gun and caliber cartridge, the buyer must choose a bullet weight. Bullet weight and shape are probably not that critical to the average deer hunter, but one should recognize that the fastest combination of powder and bullet may not always be the best. Bullet weights also affect trajectory and performance at various ranges, and bullet configuration affects what it does when it strikes home. So it is up to the hunter to find a load that is the most accurate for his rifle and does the best job in reducing a whitetail to venison.

Keep in mind one's ability to shoot a gun accurately and to hit a whitetail in a vital spot are more important than the deadliness of the cartridge used.

Ballistics tables can be confusing, but one might get some useful tips on deer guns by checking tables that give foot-pounds of energy at the ranges one expects to be shooting deer. For example, Jim Carmichael, shooting editor for Outdoor Life Magazine, has recommended that a cartridge should produce at least 1,200 foot-pounds of energy at the point of impact. If a rifle can deliver that energy up to the longest range one expects to kill at, one has a whitetail rifle.

So what about shotguns? My advice is short and sweet. I prefer an autoloader or repeating smoothbore with at least an improved-cylinder choke — nothing tighter. For one hunting exclusively with shotguns, the slug barrel is ideal. Even though the most effective shots are under 70 yards, I like the low-power scope sight simply for better vision. It's extremely important to pattern the gun at the average range one will shoot at and plan to shoot at that range — no farther. Where states allow muzzle-loaders in shotgun zones, I prefer the muzzle-loader, with scope sight. If a deer is too close, shoot it in the neck or head. Practice and you will not need to worry about a second shot.

Remember, rifles and shotguns are very personal hunting tools. Sure, listen to lots of advice, but the gun must suit you — your build, your eyes, your style of hunting and your preference for ease of handling and shooting. A number of guns that are pleasant to shoot will kill a Michigan whitetail.

Some Deer Facts and Fancy

Some years ago, I read some deer-hunting advice that cautioned against urinating at a deer stand. The idea, I gathered, was that the smell of the urine would alert an oncoming deer and spoil the hunter's chances for a shot.

Since I had been committing this no-no for years, I thought I better put it to a test. I urinated on the active deer trails I watched when bow hunting. I did so in the scrapes deer made. And I did the same on bait deer were eating. The deer didn't mind. They kept coming and I kept on killing.

I have to confess that I have clung to some handed-down beliefs for more years than I care to admit. I have learned that some are more fancy than fact and that some ought to be examined before relying on them to help tag a buck. Here are some beliefs:

*Don't walk down a deer trail to your stand.

It has never seemed to bother deer I have hunted. I walk the trails because they provide the easiest and most quiet walking. But I do wear rubber boots. And I have turned to see deer coming down the trail behind me. Maybe rubber boots is the key.

*Deer have poor eyesight.

Maybe. But don't test it by wiggling your little finger when a deer is looking at you. Deer may not easily identify a motionless hunter, but they will see you. A deer may puzzle over you or even not see you if you are still before it comes into view, but

165

deer are great at picking out movement, even the slightest — and from a distance. Biologists say they have keen eyesight.

*Still-hunt by walking so your heel or toe hits the ground first.

If you do that, your foot will make a second noise when the rest of the boot comes down. A deer's foot only makes one noise when it hits the ground. To imitate that, and I try to, a hunter should walk flat-footed. The lead foot should "feel out" any twigs that might break underfoot. This prevents extra noise.

*Noise spooks deer.

I've walked up on many a deer when making what I thought was too much noise. They spooked only after I came into sight — some, that is. Some bucks never got a chance. There are many noises in the woods, and deer like to identify them. As soon as they link a noise to humans they are gone.

But funny things happen. Slip off your safety or cock your gun when a deer can hear it and the deer can spook even when it hasn't seen you. Noise alerts deer, but their curiosity often does them in when they fail to identify the noise-maker right away.

*Always hunt upwind.

Fact is, in Michigan one can't always walk upwind. I do when I can. If you see a deer, it's foolish to try stalking it downwind. But, in Michigan, you might not get in much hunting if you let the wind dictate your route. In heavy woods or around swamps, the wind is not that important. But cross an open ridge and it could cross you up. I've had deer smell me from probably more than 100 yards away in open country. Hunt in and out of the edge of heavy cover when the wind is strong. If you always hunt up-wind, you may not get to hunt where you want to. Better to avoid the wind.

*Rut is brought on by cold weather.

If that were true, there would be no rut in regions that are warm all year. Hours of daylight more directly influence the start of the rut in northern states such as Michigan.

*Wait before following up a wounded deer.

Normally, I don't do this. If a deer is fatally wounded it is likely to die more quickly if pushed — causing continuous bleeding. Wounded deer like to lie down, seeming to sense this helps healing. Since I started bow hunting, I have followed deer wounded by archers for distances ranging from a few yards to several hundred yards, quitting when the blood trail ended or when I decided the blood lost was not enough to cause the deer problems — or quitting on finding the animal.

On its initial run a badly wounded deer may not indicate it has problems. But jump that deer and you can usually tell by the way it runs how bad off it is. If it runs as well as it did when hit, you may never get that deer. But if it shows a reluctance to run or runs weakly, just watch it and mark where it lies down. You will get it.

*Gamy meat.

Many people have asked me how to rid venison of the gamy taste. This has puzzled me because the taste of venison is what I prize. I suspect the gamy taste people refer to is the taste of venison that hasn't been properly cared for — meat that is slightly tainted.

*Washing will damage venison.

Washing out the body cavity is one of the best things you can do to a freshly killed deer. It gets rid of blood (that can taint the deer) and cools the carcass. Cooling a carcass quickly is key to having good meat.

*Hanging a deer will age it.

Hanging a deer with the hide on won't age it, my butcher friends tell me. Most of the time, a deer freezes before one gets it back from the northwoods, and a frozen deer won't age. The last word I had on aging is to skin the animal and hang it 10 days at 40 degrees.

*If you see a doe coming, watch for a buck behind it.

Well, it could happen. I've been watching does for 60 years

and only once saw a buck following one. It was the first buck I killed. But I have seen spikes or four-pointers with does in family groups in bow season.

*Deer rub their antlers to get rid of the velvet.

I think they do, but they rub trees and branches well into November — long after the velvet is gone. And this has puzzled old-timers I know who have always associated rubbing only with ridding antlers of velvet. Bucks will trash small bushes and rub bark off everything from saplings to trees with sizable diameters.

I find that where there are evergreens along the trail, bucks like to hook the overhanging limbs with their antlers. Biologists think rubs are "signposts" to other deer, partly because scents are left on the rubbed trees. I never worry over what rubs mean, I'm just grateful bucks make them so I can find out where to kill one.

*Always bleed your deer.

My grandfather always "stuck" his deer even though he usually broke the neck with his shot. So I used to do the same. It wasn't long before I noticed that little blood would come out if the deer was dead. If it isn't dead, sticking it is dangerous.(Yes, I found that out.) Since most hunters shoot their deer in the chest region, the animal is usually well bled. The bullet does the trick.

*Deer don't like to move on windy days.

The theory is that noisy woods spook deer. Maybe, but maybe not. Don't let a windy day deter you. Add to that, rain and snow and cold.

One thing is certain: A lot of bucks have been killed by hunters who didn't know you are not supposed to be out in wind, rain, snow or frigid weather.

Rinsing out the cavity with clean cold water, skinning the hide off and hanging the deer in a cool area will make the best tasting venison .

About the Author

Kenneth L. Peterson
1922 - 1997

Ken was born February 7, 1922, in Grayling, Michigan. He was drawn, at an early age, to the outdoors and its abundance of fish and wildlife. Growing up in Grayling during the twenties and thirties provided the young nimrod the opportunity to hunt small game as well as the elusive whitetail. With the legendary AuSable River practically flowing past his back door, his evolution as an expert angler and hunter was assured.

Not to be content with just hunting and fishing, he aspired to become a writer so that he could share what he experienced with others. You could say writing was in his blood since his mother, Anna, was the literary aide to the famous author, James Oliver Curwood.

After serving with the U.S. Army in Africa and Italy from 1942-1945, he returned home and enrolled in the University of Michigan. There he earned his Bachelors degree, as well as a Masters degree, in Journalism.

He began working as a reporter in 1951 for the Port Huron Times-Herald where one of his duties was that of outdoor writer. In 1954, he left Port Huron to work for The Flint Journal, where he became its outdoor editor in 1963. He held this position until his retirement in 1985.

During the course of his career he never wavered in his devotion to the outdoors. He hunted and fished in some exotic places, but always held a deep devotion for his beloved Michigan, and for his favorite game animal, the whitetail deer.

He belonged to many regional and national organizations, serving as President of the Midwest Travel Writers Association, Michigan Outdoor Writers, Flint Michigan Chapter of Trout Unlimited and National Director of Trout Unlimited.

He was editor of **Trout** magazine and a field editor of **Michigan Sportsman** magazine.

He won ten awards from the Michigan Outdoor Writers Association, Award of Merit from Michigan United Conservation Clubs, special citations from Trout Unlimited and the Ben East Award for Conservation in Journalism, plus many more. He was nominated for a Pulitzer Prize for articles on pollution.

He was a five-time Michigan duck calling champion, the Midwest duck calling champion and was runner-up in the world championship duck calling contest.

Ken lived in the country outside Davison, Michigan with Gwen, his wife of forty-nine years. Their children, Peter, Christine, and Richard, each have a career of their own.

ORDERING INFORMATION

Additional copies of MY 60 YEARS HUNTING MICHIGAN WHITETAILS may be purchased by ordering directly from:

> OUTDOOR IMAGES
> P.O. Box 250
> SUNFIELD, MI 48890-0250
> 1-800-735-3476

Name: _____

Mailing address: _____

City: _____ St.: _____ Zip: _____

Telephone: _____

Price per book: $19.95 postpaid (Michigan residents please add 6% sales tax ($1.20).

Visa and MasterCard accepted.